D0760941

STUDIES
IN THE SHAKESPEARE
APOCRYPHA

STUDIES IN THE SHAKESPEARE APOCRYPHA

BALDWIN MAXWELL

GREENWOOD PRESS, PUBLISHERS
NEW YORK

CONTENTS

ACKNOWLEDGMENTS

It is a most pleasureful duty to record my thanks to those to whom I am indebted in the preparation of these studies. My especial thanks go to Professors Allardyce Nicoll and Charles J. Sisson of the Shakespeare Institute, Stratford-upon-Avon. The studies here presented were largely written in Stratford during 1952–53 when I held the Charles Henry Foyle Research Fellowship at the Institute, and Professor Nicoll and Professor Sisson not only generously read the manuscript I thrust upon them but offered many suggestions which, had I been able to follow them all, might have made these studies more worthy of the auspices under which they were undertaken. My sincere thanks go also to the American Philosophical Society for a research grant which made possible my year in England, and to Dean Walter Loehwing of the Graduate College in the State University of Iowa for a generous grant toward publication.

BALDWIN MAXWELL

Iowa City, Iowa
December, 1955

STUDIES
IN THE SHAKESPEARE
APOCRYPHA

INTRODUCTION

THE FOUR PLAYS to be discussed in the following studies were first printed between 1595 and 1608—years during which Shakespeare must have established himself as London's most popular and successful playwright. Two of them, *The True Chronicle History of Thomas Lord Cromwell* (1602) and *The Puritan; or, The Widow of Watling Street* (1607), are upon their title-pages declared to have been written by "W. S."; a third and the earliest of the three, *The Lamentable Tragedy of Locrine* (1595), is somewhat ambiguously asserted to have been "Newly set foorth, ouerseene and corrected, by W. S." The fourth play discussed, *A Yorkshire Tragedy*, having been entered to Thomas Pavier upon the Stationers' Register on 2 May 1608, was printed for him later in the same year and is both in the Stationers' Register and on the title-page declared to have been written by "W. Shakspeare." Although the first three plays named were, of course, omitted by Heminge and Condell from the Shakespeare First Folio of 1623, by the latter half of the seventeenth century the "W. S." had been accepted as evidence of Shakespeare's authorship, and all three plays were accordingly included in the Third Shakespeare Folio of 1664, together with *A Yorkshire Tragedy* and three other plays which, though likewise omitted from the earlier folios, had previously appeared in quartos bearing Shakespeare's name.

Of this second group—the four plays which had earlier

been printed under Shakespeare's name—only *Pericles* (1609) is today accepted as in large part his. Some modern scholars have perhaps been not unwilling to recognize his hand in a few passages in *A Yorkshire Tragedy*, but none today—nor for a great many years past—has accepted it as even remotely possible that Shakespeare could have participated in any way in either *The London Prodigal* (1605) or *Sir John Oldcastle*, the latter of which had first been printed in 1599 without the ascription to Shakespeare and is, from an entry in Henslowe's *Diary*, known to have been written by four other dramatists.[1]

As Shakespeare's authorship of the three "W. S." plays is today wholly denied and as it is now recognized that his name was upon more than one occasion appended to work in which he could have had no share, it has been generally assumed that the title-page ascriptions to "W. S.," like the bolder false ascriptions to "W. Shakespeare," should be interpreted as deliberate designs on the part of the printers to capitalize upon Shakespeare's recognized superiority by misleading hesitant purchasers into thinking they were being offered plays by William Shakespeare.

Although this supposition is possibly correct, there is nevertheless much which should be considered before acceptance of the view that each of the several printers deliberately inserted the "W. S." for no reason other than the hope of increasing sales. Each of the three printers may have had a particular reason, quite different from the reasons of the others. The three appearances of "By W. S." must, however, be considered together as well as separately. The conviction of one publisher of fraud or gullibility would not, of course, prove the others similarly guilty; yet the intent of each must be considered in seeking the intent of the others. For that reason it seems preferable to explore in this preliminary chapter the possible explanations for the various ascriptions to "W. S." Doing so will also make unnecessary the great amount of repetition which would result if the problem were fully discussed in connection with each of the three plays where it arises.

The earliest of the plays bearing the initials "W. S." is *Locrine*, published by Thomas Creede in 1595. It was not Creede's invariable practice to give credit to a dramatic author. Of the ten plays printed by him and either entered to him on the Stationers' Register or published without the association of a bookseller,[2] only twice does he cite the author's name: the first play entered to him, *The Looking Glass for London* (1594), he declared written by Lodge and Greene, and he again correctly assigned *James IV* (1598) to Robert Greene. In addition to *Locrine*, two other plays published by Creede cite, both with apparent accuracy, what are claimed to be the authors' initials—Plautus' *Menaechmi* "written in English by *W. W.*" (William Warner) and *Alphonsus King of Aragon*, "Made by *R. G.*" (Robert Greene). The remaining five plays Creede published with no indication of authorship. In thus ignoring the author in half the plays he published, Creede was following what was clearly the more common practice of the time. As there were no copyright laws which assured that a playwright would be credited with work written by him or protected against the ascription to him of work by another, Creede in citing the author's initials on three of the plays was doing more than was necessary or perhaps expected. Possibly because a play was regarded as the property of the company which had bought it rather than of the author who had sold it, two-thirds of the plays printed during the six years from 1590 to 1595 have no statement concerning authorship; five (three of them printed by Creede) cite initials only; eleven carry authors' names; twenty-nine offer no hint at all of their authors' identity, although they usually name the companies which had acted them.[3] As the importance of the dramatic poet came to be more clearly recognized, this ratio is quite definitely reversed, so that during the seventeen years following the appearance of *Locrine* ninety-six plays were printed with authors' names, seventy-nine with no indication of authorship, and only thirteen with initials.

Although an examination of the thirteen plays [4] printed between 1590 and 1610 with what purport to be the authors' initials justifies little generalization, it reveals that

1. Except for the three plays published by Creede and the two plays of Marston which were printed as one undertaking by the same printer, each was from the press of a different printer.

2. Though "W. S." appears more frequently than any other initials, it was used only once by each of three different printers.

3. If we leave aside the three plays attributed to "W. S.," the initials seem in every instance to be correctly those of the author. Indeed, for at least three of the thirteen plays the poets themselves would appear to have supplied the copy (and perhaps to have suggested the manner of ascription?)—certainly for *Every Man out of his Humour* ("As it was first composed by the Author, B.I. Containing more than hath been Publickely Spoken or Acted") and presumably for *Tancred and Gismund* ("Newly reuiued and polished according to the decorum of these

dales") and for W. W.'s Englishing of the *Menaechmi* (as it presumably had never been acted).

4. For printed plays of few of the authors whose initials appeared on the playbooks had a demand been previously demonstrated. The list includes the first play to be printed by B. I(onson), I. M(arston), R. W(ilson), R. W(ilmot), W. W(arner), and the first with a title-page identifying it as the work of T. M(iddleton) or G. P(eele). Nor before *Locrine* had any printed play been ascribed to one whose initials were W. S. The names of only Greene and Chapman are to be found on the title-page of a printed play before the appearance of quartos ascribed to "R. G." and "G. C." in 1599. Except for Wilmot and Warner, however, all had been closely associated with the theatres for some years and their names were doubtless well known to those who purchased playbooks.

5. At least one of the publishers seems not to have been worried by the possibility that the initials might prove ambiguous, for "R. W." is used for both Robert Wilson and Robert Wilmot.

The last two points would seem to urge further consideration of the familiarity of Shakespeare's name, of the likelihood that "W. S." might have been used merely as the initials of a dramatist other than W. Shakespeare, and of the professional ethics of the publishers responsible for the three ascriptions to "W. S."

When *Cromwell* (1602) and *The Puritan* (1607) were published there can be no doubt that Shakespeare's name upon a printed play would have definitely assisted its sale. I suspect it would also have done so when Creede published *Locrine* in 1595, although the printers themselves seem to have been tardy in recognizing the value of his name. Before the publication of *Locrine* there had been two, possibly three, editions of *Venus and Adonis* and one of *The Rape of Lucrece*, all of course bearing Shakespeare's full name; but the only play by Shakespeare which had been printed was *Titus Andronicus*,[5] and it had been anonymous. Indeed, no printed play was to cite Shakespeare as author for at least another two years; and what may seem odd, if his initials were then thought sufficient to increase the sale of a printed play, is that within the years immediately following the appearance of *Locrine*, the quartos of *Richard II* (1597), *Richard III* (1597), *Romeo and Juliet* (1597), and *1 Henry IV* (1598) were all printed without mention of Shakespeare's authorship.

Again, since Jaggard used Shakespeare's name on *The Passionate Pilgrim* (1599) and since the title-pages of *The London Prodigal* (1605) and *A Yorkshire Tragedy* (1608) bear the name in full, one may well ask why the other publishers, especially those responsible for *Cromwell* (1602) and *The Puritan* (1607), if it were their purpose to ensnare a hesitant purchaser, did not lay a surer trap by claiming their plays to have been written by "W. Shakespeare" instead of merely by "W. S."

It was, to be sure, not uncommon during the reigns of Elizabeth and James for title-pages to cite only an author's initials. Although I am not certain that it is of real significance, it should be noted that never did the initials "W. S." appear on any authentic work by Shakespeare. His name is given on *Venus and Adonis* (1593), on *The Rape of Lucrece* (1594), on the *Sonnets* (1609). His name is attached also to *The Phoenix and the Turtle* (1601) and to "A Lover's Complaint" (1609). Only nineteen of Shakespeare's plays were printed before the appearance of the folio of 1623. Of these eleven are from their first appearance stated to have been written by "W. Shakespeare." The eight others—all early—were first printed as anonymous, but three of the eight were within a year of their first appearance reprinted under his full name. No play by Shakespeare first printed after 1600, whether in pirated or authorized text, fails to bear his name on the title-page. Yet *Cromwell* (1602) and *The Puritan* (1607) are ascribed merely to "W. S."

Unless Shakespeare were the author of *The London Prodigal* and *A Yorkshire Tragedy*, the publishers, in ascribing them to him, were obviously guilty of either error or fraud, but their guilt does not necessarily indicate similar culpability in those who assigned plays to "W. S." It is possible that the invariable use of the full name "Shakespeare" on the title-pages of all his true work was the result of a wish to distinguish between Shakespeare and another poet whose initials happened to be the same. The only instance of an unquestionable ascription to Shakespeare in which other than the full name was used is in 1611 when, twenty years after its anonymous first quarto, *The Troublesome Reign of King John* was reprinted with the claim "written by W. Sh." Here again the use of "W. Sh." may suggest that "W. S." was recognized as insufficient to distinguish William Shakespeare from another who had written for the stage.

Although no work known to be by Shakespeare bore when printed only his initials, the initials "W. S." were during the period affixed to a number of nondramatic poetical works, most of which are either definitely traceable to another or most unlikely to have been written by Shake-

speare. Much too early, of course, to have been written by
Shakespeare were the commendatory verses signed "W. S."
which appeared in Grange's *Golden Aphroditis,* 1577; nor
have any thought of ascribing to him the verses signed
"W.S." which preface Nicholas Breton's *Wil of Wit,*
1597.[6] It is impossible to say whether the sonnets in the
lost volume which was entered upon the Stationers' Register in January 1599/1600, "A booke called *Amours* by
J.D., with *certen other sonnetes* by W. S.,"[7] were indeed
sonnets by Shakespeare or were derived from the sequence
by William Smith which had been published a few years
before, *Chloris; or, The Complaint of the Passionate Despised Shepheard,* 1596. What is interesting is that when a
selection from *Chloris* appeared in *The Phoenix Nest*
(1593), it was assigned to "W. S., Gentleman," and that
in *England's Helicon* (1600) a song from *Love's Labour's
Lost* is reprinted with the ascription to "W. Shakespeare,"
while a poem from Smith's *Chloris,* "Corin's Dream of his
Fair Chloris," is assigned merely to "W. S." The author of
Chloris, however, is not known to have written for the
stage; Warburton's claim that his cook had burned a manuscript play by a "Will Smithe" called *St. George for England,* if accepted at all, is much too uncertain to permit even
attempted identification of the author.[8]

There were, however, several connected with the theatres
during the time whose initials were W. S., but unfortunately little is known about them. There was, first, William
Stanley, sixth Earl of Derby, who lived from 1561 to 1642
and who is mentioned as penning plays in 1599.[9] None of
Lord Derby's plays is extant, so far as is known, though
certain eccentrics see him as the author of the plays which,
for aristocratic reasons of his own, he arranged to be fath-

ered by the ignorant actor William Shakespeare. But Derby maintained his own company of players from 1594 to 1618, and what plays he wrote were probably acted by them. There is every reason to believe that he never wrote for the Lord Chamberlain's Men, who are said to have acted *Cromwell*, or for the Children of Paul's, who acted *The Puritan*. No company, it is true, is mentioned in connection with *Locrine*.

Another W. S. well known in the theatre was Will Sly, the great comedian. Although he has been suggested as a possible author of some of the plays ascribed to "W. S.," there exists not the slightest evidence that Sly ever attempted to write a play. Most certainly he can not have been the author of *The Puritan*, for he was both a member and a shareholder of the Chamberlain's-King's Men and any play by him, if as good as is *The Puritan*, would certainly have been acted by his company, not by their rivals. Neither is there any reason to suspect of playwriting two less known actors who bore the initials W. S.—William Smyght, "a 'player' who witnessed a loan from Philip to Francis Henslowe on 1 June 1595",[10] and William Sheppard, "a 'player' whose son Robert . . . was baptized at St. Helen's, 26 November 1602." [11]

There remain one or two W. Smiths, to whom there are very widely separated references,[12] and a Wentworth Smith, who, during the two years we hear of him, gave promise of becoming a most prolific dramatist. What is known of Wentworth Smith is only what is recorded of him in the diary of the play producer Philip Henslowe, where he is first mentioned in April 1601. In the two years between then and March 1603, when the diary comes to an end, Henslowe records payments to Smith for fifteen

plays. For only two of the fifteen, however, is Smith paid
as sole author; the others he wrote in collaboration with
one, two, or three others—with Chettle, Day, Dekker,
Drayton, Hathway, Heywood, Houghton, Munday, and
Webster. Not one of the fifteen plays for which Smith was
paid is, as far as we know, preserved; none at least is preserved under the title given it by Henslowe. We have,
therefore, no way of estimating his ability as a dramatist,
no way of knowing his interests, his tastes, or his characteristics as poet and playwright. Nor is there any indication of
what happened to him after his two years of feverish dramatic activity. Those with whom he had collaborated continued to write plays, some of them for the Chamberlain's
Men, who acted *Cromwell*, or for the Children of Paul's,
who acted *The Puritan*. So perhaps did Wentworth Smith.
But for aught we know, he may like Marlowe have died
young (although he was alive in June 1605 when he witnessed William Houghton's will),[13] or like Marston have
deserted the theatre for the ministry, or like Beaumont
have married a rich widow and retired to the life of a
country gentleman.

In 1615, however, there was published a play "Made by
W. Smith," *Hector of Germany*, "acted at the Red Bull,
and at the Curtaine, by a Companie of Young Men of this
Citie," and obviously written after the marriage of Princess
Elizabeth to the Palsgrave Frederick in 1613.[14] Although
the nature of its performance may suggest that *Hector* had
been presented by an improvised group of amateur actors,
Smith in his epistle states that "I have begun in a former
Play, called the Freemans Honour, acted by the Now-
Seruants of the Kings Maiestie, to dignifie the worthy Com-
panie of Marchantaylors." If by "now-Seruants of the

Kings Maiestie" was meant the company before it was taken under the king's patronage, there is evidence that the author of *Hector* was writing plays shortly before 1603, perhaps just when Wentworth Smith was so very active, and that at least one play by him had been acted by the Chamberlain's Men, the company which acted *Thomas Lord Cromwell*. And there may be a further reason for identifying the author of *The Freemans Honour* with Wentworth Smith in that one of the plays for which the latter was paid by Henslowe (October and November 1601) was called *The Six Clothiers*—a title which suggests that that play may also have sought to dignify one of the worthy London companies. If, however, Wentworth Smith was not the author of *The Freemans Honour*, we have evidence that, other than W. Shakespeare, not one but two dramatists with the initials W. S. were writing plays at the turn of the century.

Of the printers and booksellers concerned in the publication of the three plays assigned to "W. S.," of only one, Thomas Creede, is there other reason to suspect unethical or irregular conduct. Clear indeed appear their reputations when compared to those of the publishers who falsely ascribed plays to "W. Shakespeare." There appears no lack of evidence to support a charge of fraudulent dealing on the part of Nathaniel Butter, the publisher for whom Creede printed *The London Prodigal* in 1605, or of Thomas Pavier, who held the rights to *A Yorkshire Tragedy* and for whom it was printed in 1608. They were clearly two of the most unscrupulous publishers of their time. It was Nathaniel Butter who, in the same year in which he brought out *The Prodigal*, published Heywood's *If You Know not Me* from a pirated text declared by Hey-

wood to have been "copied only by the eare" with "scarce
one word true." [15] It was Butter and John Busby, the two
described by Sir Edmund Chambers as "the chief of the
surreptitious printers after Danter's death," [16] who published the presumably pirated first quarto of *King Lear*.
"Nor," adds Sir Edmund, "does anything we know of
Nathaniel Butter encourages belief in his *bona fides* when
he printed *The London Prodigal* without registration." [17]

The untrustworthiness of Thomas Pavier is no less established. In or shortly before 1619 Pavier with the printer
William Jaggard set about a plan which would seem to
have included the reissue of all of the available plays by
Shakespeare. Before an order from the Lord Chamberlain
to the Stationers' Company on 3 May 1619 forbade the
publication of any plays belonging to the King's Men without their consent's first being secured, only five plays had
apparently been issued—the pirated and thoroughly bad
texts of *Henry V* and *Pericles*, the horribly mutilated texts
of *2* and *3 Henry VI* as represented by *The Whole Contention*, and *A Yorkshire Tragedy*. All are, of course,
declared to have been written by "W. Shakespeare," as
were five other plays, probably already completely or par-
tially reprinted, which Pavier and Jaggard proceeded to
issue with antedated or otherwise false title-pages. Among
the latter group was *Sir John Oldcastle*, which Pavier had
previously printed without an author's name but with a
correct statement that it had been acted by the Lord Admiral's servants. It is known, of course, that *Sir John Oldcastle* was written by others. That Pavier should in 1619
claim it as a play of Shakespeare's may well increase our
suspicions of his ascription of *A Yorkshire Tragedy* to
Shakespeare in 1608 and 1619.[18]

Against those concerned in the publication of the plays assigned to "W. S.," no such strong suspicions of fraud seem warranted. As has been said, of only Thomas Creede is there other reason to suspect the integrity. The strongest case can be made for the integrity of the publisher and printer of *Cromwell,* William Jones and Richard Reed. Jones was admitted to the Stationers' Company in October 1587 and continued as a publisher until his death in 1618. He seems, however, to have been rather chary of playbooks, although one of the five printed for him must have proved extraordinarily profitable. The first play printed for him was *Edward II* in 1594, which had been entered to him in the Stationers' Register in July of the year before. The title-page correctly declares it "Written by Chri. Marlow." The second and third plays published by him, *The Woman in the Moon* (1597) and *The Blind Beggar of Alexandria* (1598), on their title-pages are correctly assigned respectively to John Lyly and George Chapman. Next he published the strangely popular *Mucedorus* (1598), which was to pass through seventeen editions by 1668, six of them printed for Jones before 1618 when his widow transferred her rights in it to another stationer. As *Mucedorus* must have proved a most profitable venture, it is surprising that Jones published but one other play, *The True Chronicle History of Thomas Lord Cromwell,* 1602, assigned on its title-page, of course, to "W. S." A possibly faulty ascription here is the only grounds for suspecting Jones's integrity; and it should be remembered that, of the five plays he published, the authors of three are correctly given and one, which must have been the most profitable, he left anonymous.

Although Jones must have possessed the rights to

Cromwell,[19] he was not himself a printer. *Cromwell* was printed for him by Richard Read. As the great majority of the manuscript playbooks which survive contain little information such as usually appeared on title-pages, and as title-pages themselves show vast differences, it is possible that when, as often happened, the rights to a play lay with the bookseller rather than with the printer, the printer may not always have been given copy for the title-page and may have been forced, at least at times, to prepare the title-page from such information as the manuscript supplied or as he himself could gather.

Richard Read, the printer of *Cromwell*, although admitted freeman of the Company of Stationers in January 1579, until he married the widow of another printer had no press of his own. Nor was he to enjoy for long either his wedded state or the printing press it brought him. His first registered publication was on 12 May 1601, his last, less than ten months later, on 24 February 1602. He printed only two plays, and both of them present difficulties. Before printing *Cromwell* he had in 1601 printed *Two Lamentable Tragedies*, assigned on its title-page to "Robert Yarington," a name nowhere else encountered in the annals of the stage. As this play seems in some way related to two lost plays which had been somewhat earlier purchased for the Lord Admiral's Men from four other dramatists, Sir Walter Greg has urged that Robert Yarington was, indeed, only "the scribe, who placed his name at the end of the MS.," whence the printer, assuming it the name of the author, transferred it to the title-page.[20] Whether such was indeed the case can probably never be known, but certainly it may be said that in ascribing *Two Lamentable Tragedies* to such an unknown pen as that of

Robert Yarington, Read had no intent of encouraging the impression that the play was by a distinguished or popular playwright. That he could have had no fraudulent intent in this instance should be borne in mind in a consideration of the ascription of *Cromwell*.

Whether or not Read mistook scribe for author in the case of Yarington, it is most improbable that he mistook for the author of *Cromwell* a scribe whose initials were W. S. Any such guess is discouraged by the same initials appearing on *The Puritan* five years later. Nor, for the same reason, can we accept for a moment the suggestion that, since *Cromwell* was acted by Shakespeare's company, the manuscript play, while under consideration by the company, may have been given him to read and that he, as one might in a modern business office, signified his approval of it by affixing his initials either at the end or on the cover.

George Elde, who published *The Puritan*, seems almost equally trustworthy. Like Read he acquired his press only upon his marriage to the widow of another printer—in Elde's case the widow of two earlier printers. Shortly after acquiring his shop and seven months before his first registered publication, Elde ran afoul the Company and was on 6 August 1604 fined 12 pence "for kepinge a prentise vnpresented contrary to order" [21]—by no means an unusual infringement of the laws of the company and one perhaps to be partly explained by the novelty of his new position as benedict and proprietor of a shop of his own. During the remainder of his career Elde seems never to have incurred the discipline of the company.

Although Elde was not primarily a printer of plays, he printed a great many, generally, however, serving

merely as printer for another bookseller to whom the plays
had been entered on the Stationers' Register and at whose
shop they were to be sold. Only four plays were entered
to his name and published by him—all four within scarcely
more than two months of 1607. The earliest of these were
two plays entered to him on the same date, 6 August, and
printed later in the year: *Northward Hoe*, which he correctly ascribed to Thomas Dekker, and *The Puritan*,
ascribed to "W. S." These were followed by two plays
entered on 7 October, *The Revenger's Tragedy*, which he
printed late in 1607 without an author's name, and *A Trick
to Catch the Old One*, likewise printed without an author's
name in 1608 but within the year reprinted with an ascription to "T. M." (Thomas Middleton). Unless it were on
The Puritan, then, Elde seems not to have made a false
ascription. That two of the four plays published by him
were first printed without indication of authorship, and
that one of them was soon afterwards reprinted with the
author's initials added, suggest that when Elde did not
know the author, he was content to publish a play without
ascription; that when he knew the author, he wished to
credit the play to him.

If, indeed, it was Elde's intent to encourage the belief
that *The Puritan* was by William Shakespeare, either he
knew surprisingly little about Shakespeare or he was remarkably careless in his plan of deceit. The title-page of
The Puritan states that it had been "Acted by the Children
of Paules." We know, of course, that Shakespeare never
wrote for Paul's boys or for any of the children's companies, that from the early 1590s on he wrote for only the
one company, that which since 1603 had been known as the
King's Men. As Shakespeare had long been an actor as well

as a playwright, it is incredible that any contemporary Londoners interested in the drama should not have known the company for which he wrote and acted. Surely no London playlover would in 1607 have taken for Shakespeare's a play which, though said to have been written by "W. S.," was further declared to have been acted by the Children of Paul's. Elde, it would seem, unless he were remarkably stupid, could hardly have been seeking to mislead the purchaser into thinking he was being offered a play by William Shakespeare.

The professional integrity of Thomas Creede, the publisher and printer of *Locrine*, is perhaps more difficult to maintain. Certainly he was in some way concerned with a number of projects which today would be strongly condemned. He was the printer of three pirated quartos of Shakespeare's plays, as well as of the falsely ascribed *London Prodigal*, but in every case save one he was merely the printer for another publisher who had perhaps secured the text. The one exception is *King Henry V*, which, in spite of an entry in the Stationers' Register, 4 August 1600(?), that its publication was "to be staied," [22] was within that year printed by Creede "for Tho. Millington and Iohn Busbey," from a piratically secured text and with no mention of Shakespeare's authorship. The explanation of their disregard of the injunction against its printing may be, as Sir Edmund Chambers suggests, that "the print of 1600 was treated as merely a reprint of the old play of *The Famous Victories of Henry V*, which was indeed to some extent Shakespeare's source, and of which Creede held the copyright." [23] But obviously Creede himself knew that the two were not the same play. Even the omission of Shakespeare's name arouses suspicions, for it is the only one of five plays by Shakespeare printed in 1600 —indeed the only play by him printed after 1598—which fails to mention his authorship. Again some deceit may be recognized in the unwarranted claim that Q3 of *Richard III*, which Creede published for Andrew Wise in 1602, presented a text "Newly augmented," when it was in fact based on Q2, which had been printed by him in 1598. Though the originator of this obvious intent to deceive may have been another, Creede must be convicted of connivance in it.

In 1595, the year in which he printed *Locrine*, Creede seems to have encountered several difficulties. On February 3 he was fined sixpence by the Stationers' Company "because hee did not appeare at the hall on the quarter daie"; and five months later, on July 7, he was fined five shillings "for hauinge kept a prentize vnpresented aboue the tyme lymitted by th[e] ordnances, and having bound and enrolled him contrarie to the same," and was required "To enter into bond in xl^{li} not to teache John Wilkynson the arte of pryntinge." [24] Presumably Creede's offence was regarded as much more serious than that for which Elde nine years later was to be fined only one shilling.

Although it must, I fear, be admitted that some of Creede's undertakings seem not above suspicion of an intent to deceive, yet it should be recalled in his defence that of the ten plays which he published independently, there is every reason to believe four correctly assigned, five bear no ascription, and only *Locrine* presents the slightest suspicion of fraud. Moreover, it is uncertain whether "W. S." is claimed to have been the author or merely the reviser; and as no printed play was to cite Shakespeare's name as author for another three years, it may be questioned whether Creede would in 1595 have recognized the power of Shakespeare's initials to stimulate sales.

Whatever the verdict rendered against Creede, and however bad were the professional ethics of Butter and Pavier, whose misdeeds were certainly not restricted to the false and wholly unambiguous ascription of plays to "William Shakespeare," it must be recognized that the evidence does not justify a confident verdict of deliberate fraud against all three publishers responsible for the ascription of plays to "W. S." There were other dramatists contemporary with Shakespeare who had those initials; there were other poets of the time actually referred to under those initials, while invariably all of Shakespeare's authentic works (and even some falsely ascribed to him) were printed only under his full name. It appears not impossible—indeed not improbable—that the ascription of one or more of the three plays printed as by "W. S." may have been accurate and without fraudulent intent. They may indeed have been written, wholly or in large part, by an author or by authors with the same initials as William Shakespeare. The substitution of the author's initials for his full name—a not uncommon practice—need not have been, although in any instance it may have been, with the intent of encouraging a mistaken identification with William Shakespeare.

1

THE LAMENTABLE TRAGEDY
OF LOCRINE

THE ARGUMENT

ACT I, Scene i. As in the first scene of each act (hereafter omitted in this synopsis) Ate enters amid thunder and lightning and, after watching the dumb show, interprets it as foreshadowing later events within the play.

Scene ii. Surrounded by his lords and kinsmen, Brutus announces that his death is near, recalls the victories he and his followers have won, and before dividing the realm among his three sons (Locrine, Camber, and Albanact), names Guendoline, daughter to his old kinsman and fellow warrior Corineus, to be the bride of Locrine. He then dies and his body is borne out to be buried in Troinovant.

Scene iii. The clown Strumbo tells the audience of his love for Dorothy, to whom he composes a love epistle which he sends her by his servant Trompart. She, returning with Trompart, accepts Strumbo's proposal, and Strumbo remains on stage to give a word of advice to any lovers there might be in the audience.

Scene iv. Locrine announces to his lords and kinsmen that, his father having now been entombed, he will this day marry Guendoline.

ACT II, Scene ii. The Scythian Humber, with his concubine (or wife) Estrild and his son Hubba, recalls the victories which have brought him to Britain and voices his hope of winning that pleasant land. His officer Segar reports that Albanact "with millions of men" approaches, meaning to give battle before morning.

Scene iii. After a song by Strumbo, Dorothy, and Trompart in praise of the pleasant life of a cobbler, a Captain enters to press Strumbo into the forces of Albanact, but Strumbo, snatching up a staff, resists until Thrasimachus, brother of Queen Guendoline, stops their fight and orders Strumbo to report for service the next day.

Scene iv. As Albanact and his lords discuss Humber's forces and the ravage they have wrought, Strumbo with Trompart runs in shouting that the Scythians have burned his home and his wife. He is comforted by Albanact's promise to build him another house near a tavern.

Scene v. Humber orders Hubba to secrete himself and a troop of horse within the wood that they may during the fight attack the Britons from their rear. Albanact and Humber exchange threats; the two armies fight and the Scythians retreat.

Scene vi. As the Britons beat back the invaders, Hubba's forces attack them from behind. Albanact, refusing to flee with the remnant of his troops, kills himself. Strumbo, who has saved his life by pretending to be slain, rises and runs out when Trompart cries "Thieves."

Scene vii. Humber exults in his victory and places the garland upon his son's brow.

ACT III, Scene ii. After Thrasimachus has reported the death of Albanact and the defeat of his army because of Hubba's cowardly attack, Camber and Corineus promise to assist Locrine in revenge.

Scene iii. As the Scythians still exult in their victory, the ghost of Albanact, invisible to them, comments on the fickleness of fortune and prophesies the early decay of Humber's glories. Segar announces that Locrine's forces are near.

Scene iv. Oliver and his son William accuse Strumbo of having meddled with Oliver's daughter Margery. Upon Strumbo's refusal to marry her, he and William fight. Margery enters to separate them but when Strumbo still refuses her marriage, she beats him until he consents.

Scene v. Locrine and his officers, near Humber's camp, promise courageous and successful fight.

Scene vi. Meeting Hubba and Segar in battle, Corineus strikes them both down with his club and presumably departs. Humber enters to lament his defeat and his need to seek some place to hide. He is followed by Albanact's ghost, which calls out for revenge.

ACT IV, Scene ii. As the Britons congratulate themselves upon their victory, soldiers lead in the captive Estrild, who laments at length her unhappy fortune. Locrine is immediately and obviously enamoured of her. Corineus, after a show of anger, seems reconciled, but warns Locrine "as thou lou'st thy life, so loue thy wife."

Scene iii. As Humber tells of his sufferings in the wilderness in which he hides, Strumbo enters and, after a comic tale, unpacks food, which the starved Humber, advancing, demands. The frightened Strumbo would give it him, but the ghost of Albanact intervenes, and Strumbo runs out followed by Humber and the ghost.

Scene iv. Locrine in soliloquy prays the gods to destroy Corineus, fear of whom has forced him to keep his beloved

Estrild for the past seven years in a secret underground palace he had built for her.

Scene v. Humber, alone, bitterly describes his suffering and then drowns himself. Albanact's ghost, which has followed, declares it can now return to the Elysian fields to report his revenge to Brutus.

ACT V, Scene ii. When Corineus' death from an old wound is announced, Locrine at once declares that he will discard Guendoline and crown Estrild queen. As Thrasimachus departs, angrily declaring he will avenge his sister, Estrild and her daughter Sabren are escorted in.

Scene iii. Thrasimachus, Guendoline, and her son Madan, entering with soldiers, vow to punish Locrine.

Scene iv. Locrine, amused that Guendoline should come in arms against him, orders his troops to march toward her camp.

Scene v. The ghost of Corineus enters amid thunder and lightning; it will "Stand a side" to "see revenge And feede [its] soule with *Locrines* ouerthrow." The opposing armies enter. Guendoline recites the wrongs done her and is mocked by Locrine and Estrild.

Scene vi. After a battle in which Locrine's forces are driven in, Locrine, entering with Estrild, recognizes that all is lost, takes his farewell, and kills himself. Estrild laments her fortune for twenty lines and then kills herself with Locrine's sword. Sabren, coming upon the bodies of her parents, is too weak to use the sword against herself, but, though captured, she escapes Guendoline's promised vengeance by drowning herself. Guendoline orders Locrine buried in his father's tomb, Estrild in a shallow grave with no honor.

Scene vii. In an epilogue Ate points the moral of the play and asks prayers for Queen Elizabeth.

Under the date of 20 July 1594 there was entered to the printer Thomas Creede in the Register of the Stationers' Company a play identified as "The lamentable Tragedie of *Locrine,* the eldest sonne of Kinge Brutus, discoursinge the warres of the Brittans &c." [1] The earliest extant quarto of this play, as it bears the date 1595, presumably appeared some months later; [2] there is no reason to suspect an earlier edition, even though on the 1595 title-page the play is declared to be there "Newlie set foorth, ouerseene and corrected, By *W. S.*" That the "Newlie set foorth" need not be interpreted as indication of a previous edition is shown by similar statements appearing on the earliest quartos of *Tamburlaine* (1590) and *A Knack to know a Knave* (1594), the former said to be "Now first, and newlie published." Neither is it likely that "ouerseene and corrected" could have been intended to claim merely that the quarto had been proofread; [3] the large number of misprints and omissions indicate that such a claim would have been wholly unjustified, as does perhaps the absence of any variants in the five copies of the quarto collated by Dr. McKerrow. [4] The simplest and most reasonable interpretation of the statement on the title-page is, certainly, that the text there printed is that of a play as it had been reworked or revised. The original need not have been an old play. [5]

There are, indeed, many and strong reasons for thinking that the text of the tragedy as it has come down to us represents a revision of an earlier play—a revision which includes the insertion of several scenes. Before one can discuss such later insertions, however, it is necessary to determine as accurately as possible the date of our present text, and as the dating of our text depends upon the sources which the dramatist can be shown to have used, I shall first discuss two hitherto unrecognized sources. The first, to be sure, offers no help in the dating, but the second, if it be accepted, may require that our text of *Locrine* be dated some years later than anyone has yet suggested.

The most comprehensive study of the sources of *The Lamentable Tragedy of Locrine* is that of Theodor Erbe, published in *Studien zur englischen Philologie* in 1904.[6] Although in all probability correct in his conclusion that the dramatist drew most heavily upon the history of Geoffrey of Monmouth, which he supplemented with the histories of Caxton and Holinshed, Erbe overlooked the drama's debt to *The Mirror for Magistrates*, not citing it as the source of any detail not found in these histories. Professor Willard Farnham later argued for the dramatist's having made some use of the *Mirror*, basing his argument principally upon the close affinity of play and mirror in a "tragic pattern and philosophy of life" which are not shared by the chronicles.[7] But Farnham offered little evidence of a more tangible sort. After noting that the forms of the proper names in the play are closer to those of the *Mirror* than to those of either Geoffrey or Caxton (but not than to those in Holinshed), Farnham recognized the "employment of a minor proper name in the form Turnus" (lines 148, 149)[8] as "the most concrete indication that in the course of his story the dramatist leaned somewhat upon the *Mirror*."

There are, however, in the very first scene of *Locrine* lines which seem unquestionably to have been inspired by

similar lines in the tragedy of Albanact in *The Mirror for
Magistrates*. The play opens with King Brutus' "latest
words" to his sons and followers as he recognizes that
his death is near—words in which he reviews their heroic
accomplishments, divides the realm among his three sons
and commands them to live in amity and in obedience to
the advice of the older councillors who have supported
him. Some of the material for the speeches in the earlier
part of the scene—those in which Brutus recalls his early
struggles and victories—could, of course, have been found
in Book I of Geoffrey, but Geoffrey offers no help to one
seeking to reconstruct the scene of Brutus' death. He
merely states most summarily at the opening of Book II
that Brutus had three sons and that "when their father
departed this life in the twenty-fourth year after his arrival,
they buried him . . . and divided the realm of Britain
amongst themselves." Caxton and Holinshed, although
they declare that Brutus divided the realm among his
three sons before his death, mention no dying speech and
are equally abrupt in telling of Brutus' death. It is only
in *Locrine* and in the story of Albanact in *The Mirror for
Magistrates* that a dying speech by Brutus is to be found;
and the speeches in these two accounts, as will be noted in
the comparisons cited below, are in remarkable agreement
both in their subject matter and in the order in which
Brutus' various observations are presented.

*Brutus' recognition of approaching death and his request
for attention to his words.*

Brutus' dying speech in the play begins by his stating
that he "draweth nigh his end,"

And I must leaue you though against my will
My sinewes shrunke, my numbed senses faile,
A chilling cold possesseth all my bones. (lines 40–42)

He thereupon commands those present—his sons and his old associates—to

. . . harken to your soueraigns latest words,
In which I will vnto you all vnfold,
Our royall mind and resolute intent . . . (lines 117–19)

In the *Mirror* Brutus, like the husbandman who provides for the future "when he perceaues the wynter colde at hande" (line 396), orders to him "His counsayle all" and his sons,

That nowe my leaue and last farewell must take:
Thus nature willes me once an ende to make:
And leave you here behinde . . . (lines 417–19)

Brutus' review of their past victories.

In both accounts there now follows a review by Brutus of the heroic struggles which have enabled the Britons to establish their new homeland—a review presented only sketchily at this point in the *Mirror* but more fully in earlier stanzas. And in the two accounts at this point there is a striking similarity not found elsewhere:

And for your sakes my *Turnus* there I lost (*Locrine*, line 148)

and

For you, at *Tours* my *Turnus* tooke his ende
(*Mirror,* line 427).

Geoffrey had written: "It chanced that a certain Trojan was there present named Turonus, a nephew of Brute's,

than whom was none more valiant and hardy save only
Corineus himself. He with his single sword slew no less
than six hundred men. Unhappily he was slain before his
time by a sudden onslaught of the Gauls; and the aforesaid city of Tours acquired the name thereof by reason of
his being there buried" (Bk. II, ch. xv). The accounts of
Caxton and Holinshed, briefer and less specific, give no
additional details. Geoffrey's "Turonus" is in Caxton and
Holinshed spelled "Turinus" or "Turin."

The spelling "Turnus," the use of the possessive pronoun, and the idea that Turnus had sacrificed himself for
his comrades are found only in the *Mirror* and in the
play.

Brutus' questioning whether his struggles were worthwhile.

In the play Brutus, after recounting his struggles in
establishing the Trojans in Britain, questions whether his
efforts have been in vain:

> Now let me see if my laborious toiles,
> If all my care, if all my greeuous wounds,
> If all my diligence were well imploid. (lines 157–59)

In the *Mirror*, in exactly the same place in the narrative,
Brutus seeks assurance that his efforts had not been in
vain:

> Nowe must I prove, if paynes were well bestowde,
> Or if I spente my gratefull giftes in vayne:
> Or if these great good turnes to you I owde,
> And might not aske your loyall loves agayne.

(lines 435–38)

Brutus' request that the lords support his sons.

In his very next speech in the play Brutus asks his "loyall peeres" to

> Fauour my sonnes, fauour these *Orphans* Lords,
> And shield them from the daungers of their foes;
>
> > (lines 178–79)

while in the *Mirror* the lords—again, of course, at the same point in the narrative—are exhorted to be to "my sonnes, that after me must raigne" "their guydes" and "their fathers, with your counsayle wise" (lines 456–65).

Division of the realm.

Exhortation to his sons to live in concord and in obedience to the advice of "these fathers grave."

In both accounts there now follows first the division of the realm by Brutus among his three sons (*Locrine*, lines 180ff., and *Mirror*, lines 470ff.), and then a final exhortation to his sons to live in concord and amity and to obey the counsels of *these fathers grave*. In the play:

> Liue long my sonnes with endlesse happinesse
> And beare firme concordance amongst your selues,
> Obey the counsels of *these fathers graue*
> That you may better beare out violence; (lines 253–56)

and in the *Mirror:*

> Firste that you take *these fathers grave* for mee,
> Imbrace their counsaile even as it were myne:
> Next that betwene your selves you will agree,

And never one at others welthe repine:
See that ye byde still bounde with frendly lyne . . .

                                        (lines 484–88)

Final blessing (or handshake) and death.

In both accounts, immediately after this final bit of advice to his sons, Brutus recognizes that death is upon him
—"My glasse is runne" (*Locrine*, line 267), "My time is
come" (*Mirror*, line 492)—speaks a final brief farewell
and dies (*Locrine*, lines 257–60 and *Mirror*, lines 491–
97).

There are, it should be noted, some verbal parallels between Brutus' death speeches as given in the *Mirror* and
in *Locrine:* "My Turnus," "For you" ("for your sakes"),
"these fathers grave." Although these parallels may be
few and slight in themselves, they would seem to assume
greater significance when it is recognized that these two
imaginative reconstructions of Brutus' dying speech—
and there are (so far as is known) but these two—not only
are strikingly similar in the ideas they express but even
present those ideas in exactly the same sequence. There is
in the death speech of Brutus as given in *Locrine* little
that is not in "The Tragedy of Albanact" in the *Mirror*—
only a somewhat fuller account of Brutus' earlier struggles and, what seems to be the dramatist's own contribu-
tion to the story, Brutus' selection of Guendoline to be
Locrine's wife; there is in Brutus' speech in the *Mirror*
nothing that does not appear in the play. Nor, unless there
were known to him some telling of the story now lost,
could the dramatist have found anywhere other than in
The Mirror for Magistrates most of what he presents in
the first scene of his play.

This indebtedness of the play to the *Mirror* offers, of course, no help in dating either the original tragedy or a revision, and for it either dramatist may have been responsible. However, the possible indebtedness of the play to another source, hitherto overlooked, may establish for our text of the play a date somewhat later than has yet been given it.

Much as the author of *Locrine* borrowed from *The Mirror for Magistrates* an effective scene not found in his principal sources, the death scene of Brutus, so he may have borrowed from another poem two other effective scenes. The scene in which Locrine first sees Estrild and that in which she, after Locrine's death, weeps over his corpse, are to be found only in the play and in *The Complaint of Elstred* by Thomas Lodge, printed with *Phillis* in 1593.[9] That the dramatist and not Lodge was the more likely borrower will, I think, be clear from an examination of the similarities in the two accounts.

The dramatist does not follow Lodge's spelling of the proper names and, indeed, differs from him in many other respects. In much the same way that he borrowed from the *Mirror* the account of Brutus' death in "The Complaint of Albanact," yet disregarded completely the following complaints of Locrine and Elstride, the dramatist perhaps took from Lodge's poem hints for two scenes only.

The first meeting of Locrine and Estrild.

Of the first meeting of Locrine and Estrild only three of the extant accounts—the two under discussion and the complaint of Elstride in *The Mirror for Magistrates*—give any details beyond the mere statement that Estrild was taken captive in Locrine's victory over Humber or

that, after the battle, she (often with two other women)
was discovered in one of Humber's ships. In *The Mirror
for Magistrates* Elstride declares that her beauty and unhappiness "did cause them," apparently some Britons of
nobleness and pity,

> for my sake
> Mee to commende, unto their noble Kinge,
> Who wilde they should me into presence bringe.

(lines 68–70)

In the play, on the other hand, she is not brought to
Locrine by those who have sympathy for her but is
dragged before him by two base soldiers who, even in the
king's presence, quarrel as to which of them is her captor
(line 1491ff.). A similar selfishness and, certainly, no
sympathy prompted her captors in Lodge, who makes
Elstred say

> I was presented by unhallowed hand,
> To stoute *Locrinus* King of *Logiers* land. (stanza 31)

Although Lodge's casual mention of "unhallowed hand"
may suggest that it is he who is responsible for whatever
borrowing there may be, later similarities urge that the
two base soldiers are more likely the dramatist's development of the suggestion in Lodge.

Only in Lodge and in the play is mention made of
Estrild's weeping when brought before Locrine. In the
play the king himself testifies to her weeping:

> With floods of woes she seems orewhelmed to bee.

(line 1459)

.   .   .   .

> If she haue cause to weepe for *Humbers* death,
> And shead sault teares for her ouerthrow. (lines 1462–63)

In Lodge Elstred states that,

> Him when I saw, I shooke, and shaking wept,
> And weeping, to his throne for mercy crept. (stanza 32)

A final similarity in the two accounts of this first meeting is that they alone present a situation in which the captive pleads for mercy from a captor who is himself immediately a prisoner of love. Although Locrine in many of the other accounts falls in love at his first sight of Estrild, the implication in all of them is that he saw, he loved, he took. In the play and in Lodge's poem, however, at this first meeting of the two, they are both overwhelmed by woe, she for her unhappy fortune, he for his love. In Lodge Elstred recalls that

> . . . whilst I rent my carelesse-scattered locks,
> Those tricked trammels where true love was tangled,
> At *Locrins* breast for mercy fancie knocks,
> Shadowed in seemely lookes where-with love angled:
>   And when I cry'd, O pitty me my King,
>   His eyes cry'd pitty me, by woe looking. (stanza 33)

What is in the poem related in retrospect is, of course, in the play presented on the stage. As Estrild weeps her change of fortune, Locrine "at one side of the stage" tells the effect her beauty and grief have on him:

> If she haue cause to weepe for *Humbers* death,
> And shead sault teares for her ouerthrow,
> *Locrine* may well bewaile his proper griefe,
> *Locrine* may moue his owne peculiar woe,
> He being conquerd died a speedie death, . . .
> I being conqueror, liue a lingring life,
> And feele the force of *Cupids* suddaine stroke.

I gaue him cause to die a speedie death,
He left me cause to wish a speedie death . . .

(lines 1462–71)

No other account suggests Locrine's suffering because of
his sudden love.

Estrild's weeping over the corpse of Locrine.

That this similarity in the treatment of the first meeting of Locrine and Estrild may be more than coincidental
is urged by a second scene or situation common only to
Lodge's poem and the play—that in which Estrild, after
his defeat by the forces under Queen Guendoline, laments
the slaying of King Locrine. In the poem Elstred, with
her young daughter, had searched the battlefield until
she found Locrine's body and then lamented at length
her second bereavement (stanzas 68–72); in the play,
where Locrine dies upon his own sword rather than by an
enemy's arrow, Estrild enters with Locrine and, after he
dies and before she kills herself with the same sword,
laments his death for twenty lines.

The development of these two situations peculiar to
Lodge and the dramatist—the first appearance of Estrild before King Locrine and her lament after his defeat
and death—are, one might say, just the sort of elabora-
tion to be expected when their story is more fully told
with direct discourse in a narrative poem or a play. To some
extent that is undoubtedly true; but it should be remembered that neither of these situations is described or presented in the complaint of Elstride in *The Mirror for
Magistrates,* where it is merely said that, immediately
after Locrine's death, Elstride "to late, began in vayne
to flye" (line 211).

There is another reason for thinking that the dramatist
made use of Lodge's poem, and that it is hardly feasible
to seek to explain the similarities peculiar to their accounts
by assuming that Lodge and the dramatist knew and made
use of some telling of the story now unknown, for such an
assumption would seem to require other assumptions—
that the lost account was, like Lodge's, a complaint and
that it was, furthermore, even written in the same stanza
form which Lodge was to use. Not only do Estrild's
speeches in these two scenes of the play constitute a complaint, but the lines in the first of the two episodes are
sharply set apart from the other lines of the play. Except
in this one episode there is remarkably little rime in *The
Tragedy of Locrine*. Few scenes even end in rimed couplets.
Only twice elsewhere in the play are there instances of alternate rime, and one of these four lines is borrowed from
Spenser's *Visions of the World's Vanity*. When, however,
in IV, ii, Estrild is brought in captive, her first speech, one
of thirty lines, consists of five six-line stanzas of iambic
pentameter riming *a b a b c c*—the favorite stanza of Lodge,
which he used throughout his *Complaint of Elstred*. Estrild's second and third speeches in the scene, taken with
two speeches of Locrine, constitute another such stanza,
while in the intervening speech of Locrine there appear one
perfect and two imperfect instances of the same stanza
form.

On the other hand, it should be noted that no verbal
similarities appear in play and poem—a fact which is perhaps puzzling if the dramatist made use of Lodge's poem,
for few if any of the plays of the period borrowed more
freely than did *Locrine* the wording of other plays and
poems. Witness especially the transfer of lines from
Spenser and the large number of verbal parallels which

have been noted in the plays of numerous authors. Clearly
the dramatist seems not to have written with Lodge's poem
beside him; possibly he read it while it was still in manuscript and then passed it along or returned it to its author.
But I find it difficult to believe that he had not at some
time seen it, for it would appear a coincidence a bit too
remarkable if, when rime is so rare elsewhere in the play,
the dramatist should have independently used Lodge's
stanza, common though that stanza be in the period, only
for material found in no other telling of Estrild's story than
Lodge's complaint.

Neither *Phillis* nor *The Complaint of Elstred* was entered upon the Stationers' Register. They were first
printed, so far as is known, by John Busbie in 1593 under
the title *Phillis: honoured with pastorall sonnets: where-
vnto is annexed the tragicall complaynt of Elstred*. Although it is possible that the dramatist responsible for our
text of *Locrine* may have read Lodge's poem before it was
published, it is perhaps safer to assume, at least tentatively,
that he knew it in its printed form. To do so does not neces-
sitate a radical change in the accepted dating of the play.
Locrine, having been entered on the Stationers' Register
on 20 July 1594, appeared in a quarto bearing the date
1595. Because of its versification, its bombast, its crude
plotting, and its use of the conventions of early Senecan
revenge tragedy, as well as because of a supposed reference
to the plots of Mary Queen of Scots,[10] early critics confidently assigned *Locrine* to the years 1585–1586. When,
however, it was shown, first, that in the play as printed
there are a considerable number of lines lifted from
Spenser's *Complaints* [11] (printed 1591) and, second, that
in certain respects the play agrees with no extant version of

the Locrine saga other than that told in Book II of *The Faerie Queene*,[12] it became necessary to accept a date no earlier than 1591 or, as does Sir Edmund Chambers, "c.1591." To recognize, as perhaps we should, that *The Tragedy of Locrine* reveals the influence also of *The Complaint of Elstred* requires only that the date of the present text, apparently a revision, be set some two years later, in 1593, if the redactor knew the printed poem; perhaps no later than "c. 1591" if there is reason to believe he may have known the poem while it was still in manuscript.

There are, as has been said, strong reasons for thinking that our present text of *Locrine* represents a revision. The descriptive title given on the title-page, as it is identical to that which appears at the head of the first page of text, may well have been the title in the manuscript from which the printer worked. The full title reads: "The Lamentable Tragedie of *Locrine*, the eldest sonne of King *Brutus*, discoursing the warres of the *Britaines*, and *Hunnes*, with their discomfiture: *The* Britaines *victorie with their Accidents, and the death of* Albanact." This title is repetitive and misleading and, despite its length, quite inadequate, making no reference to the events of the last two acts, which in the play, as in all earlier versions of the Locrine story, are recognized as the really eventful happenings of Locrine's reign: his love for Estrild, whom he secretly kept for seven years before daring to discard Guendoline and to crown queen; and Guendoline's revenge, with the resulting deaths of Locrine, Estrild, and their daughter Sabren. The latest event in the play referred to in the title is the defeat of the Huns, which takes place in Act III, while the death of Albanact, given surprising emphasis in the title, occurs well before the end of Act II. That so inapt and inadequate a descriptive title could have been prepared by the author of the play himself can be credible only if it were his original intention, perhaps soon abandoned, to present the story in two separate plays, the first part to end with the defeat of the Huns and the second part to deal with the love of Locrine and Estrild and Guendoline's revenge upon them. There appearing at different times in the play two ghosts demanding revenge upon different persons renders each ghost less effective. Were the story presented in two plays, the ghost of Albanact could have sought and secured his revenge upon Humber in Part I, leaving Part II to the ghost of Corineus.

But in the play that has come down there seems hardly sufficient material from which to build two plays. Many stage directions are omitted, several times no method is suggested for removing corpses from the stage, possibly some passages are printed out of place, but no essential step in the story seems lacking; the only reported action is the death of Corineus. Certainly there are insufficient grounds for assuming that our text of Locrine represents two plays which have been telescoped into one. Unless, however, the author was at times exceptionally confused and prone to forgetfulness, the text must have suffered from a careless or indifferent redactor. There are contradictions and confusions which cannot be explained either by the printer's lack of skill or by the illegibility of the papers from which he worked. It is interesting and worthy of note that most of these contradictions and confusions appear in characters and incidents which are not to be found in any earlier version of the story. Justifiable, certainly, are the liberties taken by the dramatist to bind the characters of the play more closely together. Corineus is throughout unfaithfully presented as brother to King Brutus. The position of Assaracus is more confused. In the sources he was a Greek whom Brutus knew only after his exile. When in I, ii, Brutus speaks of "old *Assarachus* mine eame" (line 123), he perhaps need not refer to the Assaracus of the play, who seems to claim Brutus as a brother when he speaks of Corineus as "by [*for* my] brother" (line 1796); Locrine's addressing Assaracus as "uncle" (line 1881) would fit either relationship.

Of the British characters presented in the play, the only one not mentioned in the sources is Thrasimachus, who in the play is the son of Corineus and the brother of Guendoline. He is one of many characters in Elizabethan drama upon whom passing years seem to have little effect; indeed he seems to grow younger as the play progresses, so that one is tempted to suggest that he has absorbed a part not originally his—that two distinct parts have been combined into one. In I, ii, with such elder statesmen and warriors as Corineus, Assaracus, and Debon on the stage, there seems no reason why the dramatist should elect to allow Thrasimachus, unless he regarded him as one of the leaders, to protest to Locrine, "in the name of all" "your loyall peers," to accomplish aught that may ease the old king's grief (line 106ff.), or to be the one to speak to Locrine for "your subjects euery one" in I, v. Presumably he is one of the leaders supporting Albanact against Humber in Act II and Locrine against Humber in Act III. Although some of the earlier accounts give the duration of Locrine's reign as twenty years, the play seems to follow Geoffrey of Monmouth in allowing him but ten

years. The only definite statement in the play is that seven
years passed after the defeat of Humber before Locrine
casts aside Queen Guendoline (line 1683). When Thrasimachus, as the leader of his sister's forces, meets Locrine
before the final battle, the modern reader (I am less sure
of the Elizabethan) may be surprised by the king's addressing as "Thou beardlesse boy" (line 1840) one who
had seemed to be a leader and warrior seven or more
years before, and especially surprised by Thrasimachus in
his reply speaking of himself as "young and of a tender
age" (line 1844).

It may be noted, too, that in the same speech in which
Thrasimachus speaks of his tender age he is made to confuse the enemies his father had overcome. In lines 1846–
47 he recalls that

> My noble father with his conquering sword,
> Slew the two giants kings of *Aquitaine*.

In Aquitaine, as Brutus had stated in lines 144ff., the
Britons had overcome the Gauls under Goffarius and his
brother Gathelus (who were no giants), and

> From thence vpon the strons of *Albion*
> To *Corus* hauen happily we came,
> And queld the giants, come of *Albions* race,
> With *Gogmagog* sonne to *Samotheus*
> The cursed Captaine of that damned crew . . .

Perhaps "Aquitaine" was merely a slip of the pen or represents a printer's substitution for "Albion," but the "two
kings" urges that the writer was thinking not of giants
under Gogmagog but of Goffarius and Gathelus.

Next, one is puzzled by the pronouns in the speech with

which Locrine opens scene v of Act III, the scene immediately preceding the battle between his forces and those under Humber. In this speech of twenty-one lines appear the following:

> Now cursed *Humber* doth *thy* end draw nie,
> Downe goes the glorie of *his* victories,
> And all *his* fame, and all *his* high renowne
> Shall in a moment yeeld to *Locrines* sword,
> *Thy* bragging banners crost with argent streames,
> The ornaments of *thy* pauillions
> Shall all be captiuated with this hand,
> And *thou thy* selfe at *Albanactus* tombe
> Shall offred be in satisfaction
> Of all the wrongs *thou* didst him when he liu'd.
>
> (lines 1229–38)

Why the shift from "thy" to "his" in the second and third lines? Humber himself is not on stage; so it cannot be that the remainder of the speech is addressed to him and the three lines (2–4) are spoken as Locrine turns from Humber to address his followers. The three lines add little or nothing, and, with them omitted, the first line reads smoothly with lines 5 and following.

Evidence for a similar but more extensive insertion of lines is to be seen in Act IV. As the Britons are exulting after the defeat of Humber, Locrine remarks in lines 1423–24:

> But staie, mee thinkes I heare some shriking noise,
> That draweth neare to our pauillion,

and there follows the stage direction "Enter the souldiers leading in *Estrild*." The soldiers, however, are not ques-

'tioned nor do they speak until sixty-five lines later, when
one of them explains:

> My Lord, in ransacking the Scithian tents
> I found this Ladie, and to manifest
> That earnest zeale I beare vnto your grace,
> I hear present her to your maiestie. (lines 1491–94)

Were the intervening lines of dialogue omitted, the action
of the scene would develop logically and smoothly; included, they both retard the action of the scene and fail
completely to blend with the style in which the rest of
the play is written. As the soldiers stand awkwardly by,
unable to manifest their earnest zeal, there are sixty-five
lines of speeches by Estrild and Locrine which develop
the situation already discussed as peculiar to Lodge's
Complaint and the play. Estrild first speaks her complaint,
five six-line stanzas of iambic pentameter verse, riming
a b a b c c; Locrine delivers a soliloquy of twenty-four
lines in which there appears one perfect example of the
same stanza as well as other couplets and alternate rimes;
and finally, before the soldier is permitted to explain, Estrild and Locrine, in two speeches each, combine to present another such stanza. As the action of the scene is
awkwardly interrupted, as this use of rime appears nowhere else in the play, and as the situation of the weeping
Estrild and the suddenly love-sick Locrine seems to have
been borrowed from Lodge, there would appear to be strong
reason for declaring most of these sixty-five lines an insertion into a scene previously written. Such a view may
find some support, too, from the fact that it is only in this
scene that Estrild is presented as Humber's wife and queen;

elsewhere throughout the play she is called his concubine or paramour.[13]

The strongest evidence of revision, however, is to be found in one of the comic scenes. The comedy of the play is seldom woven into and never really integrated with the main plots. The first comic scene, I, iii, does, to be sure, serve an important purpose in allowing an interval between the death of Brutus in I, ii, and Locrine's announcement in I, iv, that, his father being now entombed, he will this day solemnize his marriage to Guendoline. The comedy in scene iii is derived from a monologue by Strumbo, who uses a Spanish phrase and signs himself "Signor Strumbo," reveals a fondness for "new coined wordes" and the phrase "not onlie but also," and, to support his learning in astrology, cites the fourth book of *Consultations* by Lactantius.

The next comedy is to be found in II, iii, where Strumbo appears as a shoemaker, and with his new wife Dorothy and his man Trompart sings a jolly song in praise of the cobbler's merry life. The comic element is now first joined to the serious action of the play when a Captain enters to press Strumbo into the army. The cobbler, "snatching vp a staffe," fights with the Captain until Thrasimachus enters to stop the fight and to repeat the captain's command that Strumbo "appeare to morrow in the towne-house of *Cathnes*" (lines 628–29, 656). In the following scene Strumbo and Trompart burst in upon Albanact and his generals, "crying often," the stage direction reads, "wilde fire and pitch!" to report that their house and others have been burned by the Scythians. By introducing the comedy of these two scenes the dramatist perhaps sought again

to suggest the passing of time and to increase suspense by
delaying the battle between Humber and Albanact. He
has succeeded, however, only in confusing both the time
sequence and the setting of scene iv. In scene ii Segar
(lines 523–24), Hubba (lines 538–41), and Humber
(lines 553–55) all declare the battle will take place at day-
break the following day. In scene iii Strumbo is ordered
to report for induction "to morrow in the towne-house of
Cathnes." The opening of scene iv seems so clearly to
suggest the imminence of the battle that in his edition of
the play Mr. Tucker Brooke denotes the setting as *"The
camp of* Albanact." When, however, Strumbo and Trompart run in shouting "wilde fire and pitch," they are repri-
manded by Thrasimachus, who demands

> What sirs what mean you by these clamors made,
> Those outcries raised in our stately court.

(lines 707–08) [14]

Similar disregard of time and place is, of course, frequent
in Elizabethan plays, and is of significance here only in
view of other inconsistencies apparently occasioned by the
introduction of the comic scenes.

Except for the scene in which Strumbo appears with
Humber, to be discussed later, this is the last time that
anything like integration is achieved of the comic and the
serious characters. The clowns reappear, to be sure, in each
of the two following scenes, but either they are alone upon
the stage, as at the end of scene vi, or their few speeches
are wholly ignored by those on stage with them.

The next comic scene, III, iv, is unrelated either to the
serious plot or to any of the previous comic scenes of the

play. Trompart's presence is noted in the opening stage direction but he remains mute, and the action concerns the beating by which Margerie, after her father and brother have failed, convinces Strumbo that he must take her to wife.

It is in the final comic scene of the play that there is, I believe, strong indication that the play has been tampered with—I should not say "corrected." This is Act IV, scene iii, in which Strumbo meets the defeated Humber. In all the earlier accounts of the story Humber is said to have drowned immediately after the battle with Locrine, some times in an attempt to escape the Britons and at other times in an act of despair. In the play the battle is rather summarily treated. After an alarum is sounded, "Enter *Hubba* and *Segar* at one doore, and *Corineus* at the other (line 1278)"; there is a brief exchange of boasts and then Corineus "Strikes them both downe with his club" (line 1294) and presumably goes out, though his exit is unmarked. Humber enters cursing Locrine and his own fate:

> . . . damned be the gods & starres
> That did not drowne me in faire *Thetis* plaines.
> Curst be the sea that with outragious waues
> With surging billowes did not riue my shippes
> Against the rocks of high *Cerannia*,
> Or swallow(ed) me into her watrie gulfe.

(lines 1321–26)

Here the Ghost of Albanact enters and Humber, after speaking of

> . . . the burning furie of that heate
> That rageth in mine euerlasting soule, (lines 1348–49)

runs out, followed by the Ghost's cry "Vindicta, vindicta."

Had the dramatist followed his sources, Humber would at this point have drowned himself, and his speeches just quoted seem to prepare the way for his doing so. Indeed, one has no doubts that Humber has found such an escape from his suffering when at the opening of the following scene Locrine, reviewing the battle, declares

> Now cursed *Humber* hast thou payd thy due. (line 1388)

> With losse of life, and euerduring shame. (line 1391)

Later in the scene, after the weeping Estrild is led in, Locrine, at once suffering the pangs of love, declares that

> If she haue cause to weepe for *Humbers* death . . .
> *Locrine* may well bewaile his proper griefe . . .
> He being conquerd died a speedie death,
> And felt not long his lamentable smart,
> I being conqueror, liue a lingring life . . .
> I gaue him cause to die a speedie death,
> He left me cause to wish a speedie death. (lines 1462–71)

And as Locrine presses his suit, Estrild asks:

> How can he fauor me that slew my spouse? (line 1508)

> . . . *Locrine* was the causer of his death. (line 1510)

> But he [Humber] was linckt to me in marriage bond,
> And would you haue me loue his slaughterer?
>
> (lines 1513–14)

Although all but the first of these quotations are from that portion of Act IV, scene ii, which I have suggested was inserted by a reviser, they agree both with what we are told in lines 1388–91 and with what is reported in all earlier accounts of the battle.

But in spite of these confidently uttered and certainly not unexpected statements that Humber has died, he reappears in the next scene in a bit of comedy very similar, as has often been noted, to a comic scene in *Selimus* (lines 1900ff.). Far from having "died a speedie death," he appears not even seriously wounded. Suffering the pangs of hunger, he has found

> . . . not a roote, no frute, no beast, no bird,
> To nourish *Humber* in this wildernesse. (lines 1586–87)

During his complaints the clown Strumbo enters and, sitting down, pulls out "his vittailes." At Humber's threats, Strumbo agrees to share his food, but, as the stage direction instructs:

Let him make as though hee would giue him some, and as he putteth out his hand, enter the ghoast of *Albanact*, and strike him on the hand, and so *Strumbo* runnes out, *Humber* following him. (lines 1669–73)

The next two scenes render even more remarkable the changes which the play has introduced into the story of Humber. In the first of these scenes (IV, iv) Locrine, in agreement with all the sources, declares that for seven years Corineus has lived "To *Locrines* griefe, and faire *Estrildas* woe," thus indicating how much time has elapsed since Humber's overthrow. In the following scene, however, Humber again appears and before "Fling[ing] himself into the riuer" (line 1756) tells of the misery he has suffered "for feare and hunger," thinking

> at euery boisterous blast
> Now *Locrine* comes, now *Humber* thou must die—
> (lines 1729–30)

in the present text a baseless fear, it would seem, for Locrine never expresses doubts of his earlier conviction that
Humber died at the time of the battle.

All told, the curses and laments uttered by Humber in
the three scenes in which he appears after his defeat amount
to 128 lines, lines abounding in repetitious thoughts and
phrases. As there are (omitting the dumb shows and their
explanations) fewer than 2,000 lines in the entire play,
it is obvious that the dramatist lost all sense of time, pro-
portion, and importance in making this addition to his
sources, or that Humber's original laments have been first
divided and then elaborated—presumably to permit the
introduction of the comedy of IV, iii.

The latter is, I suspect, the correct explanation. It is
quite impossible to say whether this or any other of the
comic scenes presents Strumbo in or out of character, for
he has no peculiar character of his own, but rather, like
the usual comedian of his day, he in each scene assumes
the character demanded by the situation in which he is
placed. On his earlier appearances he has been in turn
Signor Strumbo, an approximation of the fantastical gull-
pedant, next the merry and manly cobbler, then the
frightened clown who is reconciled to the loss of his house
(and wife) by the hope for a new house nearer a tavern,
then the unwarlike simpleton forced to masquerade as a
soldier, who utters a boast and then to escape injury pretends to be slain, and, finally, the lusty young bachelor,
unwilling to wed, whose mind is changed by the blows of
a determined shrew. His roles are as unlike as they are,
every one of them, conventional.

It is not to be argued, however, that the comic incident
involving Strumbo and Humber was inserted into *Locrine*

at a later date than were the other comic scenes of the play. Yet it cannot be doubted that the inclusion of this incident is the cause of the awkward and absurd departure from all earlier accounts, requiring of Humber seven years of flight and three scenes, instead of one, in which to bewail his woes. Moreover, there is what I take to be evidence that the Humber-Strumbo scene, and perhaps the other comic scenes as well, were not written by the same author as were the serious scenes of the play. With but few exceptions, whenever in the comic scenes one speaks immediately upon his entrance, to the stage direction indicating his entrance there is appended "saying," "saith," or the like:

Enter *Strumbo* aboue in a gowne, with inke and paper in his hand, saying (lines 309–10)

Trompart entring saith (line 361)

Enter *Strumbo, Dorothie, Trompart* cobling shooes and singing [the song follows at once] (lines 569–70)

Enter *Strumbo* and *Trompart,* crying often (line 705)

Albanact enter and say, clownes with him (line 779)

Enter *Strumbo* with a pitchforke, and a scotch-cap, saying (lines 1596–97)

Only once in the play proper is this type of stage direction used when not noting the entrance of the comic characters. At the opening of IV, v, there appears "Enter *Humber* alone, saying" (line 1721); but that is the scene in which Humber at long last drowns himself, the scene which seems to have been transferred from its logical place, immediately after the battle, in order to permit the comedy with Strumbo in IV, iii. If the writer of the comic scenes made such a transfer, it is to be expected that his peculiar type of stage direction would here be used in a scene constructed by him of a portion from one of the earlier scenes in which Humber had bewailed his misfortunes. Furthermore, although there are, of course, a great many more entrances in the serious parts of the play than there are in the comic parts, never is this type of stage direction found elsewhere in the play proper. It is, however, twice found at the end of dumb shows, those preceding Acts II and IV, the descriptions of both of which close with the same words: "*Ate*, remaining, saying." (Interestingly, neither of these introduces either of the speeches of Ate which have been shown to have been constructed largely of lines borrowed from Spenser.)

If there was such tampering with the text of *Locrine* as I have suggested, it need not, of course, have been that of a reviser several years after the play's original composition, although the nature of the tampering seems to rule out a true and complete collaboration of two authors. It could, however, have resulted from the actors' belief that an earlier draft of the play, recently acquired by them, needed a larger amount of comedy either to be successfully performed or to take full advantage of the abilities of the company's comedians, and their resulting decision to hire some other writer to insert additional comic material. Some such explanation as this would, I think, seem quite satisfactory were we to consider only the internal evidence presented by the text of *Locrine* itself; but such an explanation may be rendered less acceptable by the uncertain connection which *Locrine* bears to *Selimus* in both its serious and its comic parts. If, to be sure, the author of

Selimus drew from *Locrine,* as seems to be the more widely held view today, and drew from it in what may be called its expanded form, the relationship of the two plays would present no difficulty in the acceptance of the above explanation.

But I must confess to some uncertainty as to just what may have been the relationship of the two plays. Attention was first called to this relationship by P. A. Daniel, who in a brief note to the *Athenaeum,* 16 April 1898, observed that several passages in the two plays were practically identical. About three years later Charles Crawford again called attention to the similar passages in the two plays, and noted that among them were several passages which had been lifted from Spenser's *Complaints.*[15] Thinking he recognized a difference in the use made of Spenser's lines in the two plays—the author of *Locrine,* he thought, sought to vary Spenser's language while the author of *Selimus* was content not to vary it—Crawford concluded that *Locrine* borrowed from *Selimus.* In 1905 Emil Koeppel published in the *Jahrbuch der deutschen Shakespeare-Gesellschaft* [16] the result of his study of the parallels cited by Crawford, a study in which he reached the opposite conclusion; viz., that *Selimus* borrowed from *Locrine.* Koeppel's conclusion was strongly supported by J. W. Cunliffe in *The Cambridge History of English Literature,* whose argument was largely based on the then unpublished study by Frank G. Hubbard. When later Hubbard's study was published,[17] it seems to have established the view that the author of *Selimus* was the borrower.

To Hubbard's examination of the similar comic scenes, with which he began his argument, I shall return later. "Much stronger proof that *Selimus* borrows from *Locrine* can be drawn," he declared, "from a consideration of the material in the two plays that has been taken from Spenser's *Complaints*." One passage in *Locrine* (lines 803–20), Hubbard notes, is largely made up of lines borrowed from two passages not far apart in Spenser's *Ruins of Rome*, between which the dramatist has (unless he borrowed them from *Selimus*) inserted lines of his own. Eight of these lines appear also in *Selimus*, but in two separate passages far apart (lines 415–16 and 2421–29), the second of which is composed of "one line from Spenser and five original with *Locrine* (or *Selimus*)," while "in *Locrine* all the lines under consideration occur in one connected passage." Mr. Hubbard argues thus:

If we assume that *Selimus* is copied by *Locrine* here, we are compelled to believe that the author of *Locrine* made up the passage in question of two passages from *Selimus* far apart, a passage from the *Ruines of Rome* not used by the author of *Selimus*, and inserted lines of his own. It is surely much more probable that the author of *Locrine* borrowed from two passages of the *Ruines of Rome*, inserting lines of his own, and that the author of *Selimus* borrowed lines from *Locrine*, putting them in two parts of his play. This probability becomes almost a certainty when we remember that *Selimus* has nothing from Spenser's *Complaints* (with the possible exception of a single line) not found in *Locrine*, while *Locrine* has much from the *Complaints* not found in *Selimus*.[18]

This is a strong argument and has, I believe, convinced nearly all critics. After noting *Locrine's* indebtedness to a line in Greene's *Menaphon* ("the arme-strong darling of the doubled night"), Hubbard quotes three passages from *Locrine* and one from *Selimus* (the italics are Hubbard's):

The *armestrong offspring* of the doubted [doubled] knight,
Stout Hercules Alcmenas mightie sonne,
That tamde the monsters of the threefold world.

(Locrine, lines 1253–55)

Stout Hercules the mirrour of the world,
Sonne to Alcmena and great *Iupiter*,
After so many conquests wonne in field,
After so many monsters queld by force,
Yeelded his valiant heart to *Omphale*.

(Locrine, lines 1362–66)

Now sit I like the mightie god of warre,
When, armed with his coat of Adament.

(Locrine, lines 1225–26)

Now sit I like the arme-strong son of Ioue
When after he had all his monsters quell'd,
He was receiu'd in heauen mongst the gods,
And had faire Hebe for his louely bride.

(Selimus, lines 1671–74)

"The perfectly natural inference to be drawn from an examination of these passages is," wrote Hubbard, "that the author of *Locrine* borrowed from Greene, amplified the material borrowed, and passed some of it on to *Selimus*." He thought it "absolutely unreasonable to infer that the author of *Locrine* developed his lines from the suggestions contained in the passage in *Selimus*." [19]

On these passages I think Hubbard's argument less convincing. The ability to amplify and develop is one of the chief vices of the author of *Locrine,* while Hubbard's suggestion that the author of *Selimus* brought together into a single passage words and ideas from the three separated passages in *Locrine,* appears to weaken to

no slight degree his argument concerning the earlier passage discussed. But let us turn to the comedy common to
both plays.

In *Locrine*, IV, iii, Humber in a soliloquy of twenty
lines tells how his entrails burn for want of drink, his
bowels cry for food. Strumbo enters and addresses to the
audience a report of his married life, telling how on his
return home his wife, a fagot stick in her hand, had demanded, "Thou drunken knave where hast thou bin so
long?" Although he "trembled fearing she would set her
ten commandments" in his face, he had found a way to
please her. He then sits down and pulls out his victuals.
After further complaint by Humber, Strumbo, discovering
him, pockets his food and seeks to hide himself, but seeing
the food, Humber exclaims:

> O *Iupiter* hast thou sent *Mercury*
> In clownish shape to minister some foode?
> Some meate, some meate, some meate. (lines 1655–57)

"O alasse sir," cries Strumbo, "ye are deceiued, I am
not *Mercury*, I am *Strumbo*." Frightened, he would share
his food, but the Ghost of Albanact, entering, strikes his
wrist and he runs out followed by Humber.

In *Selimus* the shepherd Bullithrumble in a soliloquy
says he lives "in daily feare of the breach of my wiues
ten-commandments"; he knows not how to please her:

> When from abroad I do come in,
> Sir Knaue she cries, where haue you bin?

When that morning his wife came with a holly wand and
blest his shoulders, he had run away, he says, and will now
"sit downe and eate my meate." As he is eating, Corcut

enters with his page and, before seeing Bullithrumble, laments for thirty lines the cruelty of his brother Selimus, to escape capture by whom he had fled from Magnesia to Smyrna, where Bostangi Bassa, Selimus' son in law, so closely guarded the coast that, says Corcut:

> These two dayes haue we kept us in the caue,
> Eating such herbes as the ground did affoord;
> And now through hunger are we both constrain'd
> Like fearefull snakes to creep out step by step,
> And see if we may get vs any food.
> And in good time, see yonder sits a man,
> Spreading a hungry dinner on the grasse. (lines 1936–42)

Bullithrumble, spying them, puts away his meat. When Corcut calls to him "Haile groome," the shepherd replies "Good Lord sir, you are deceiued, my names master Bullithrumble." When Corcut beseeches him by the blessed Christ to "Giue some meate to poore hunger-starued men," Bullithrumble agrees to take the prince and his page as his servants. As the others go off for food, the page steals away to win reward by betraying his master.

On the similarity of the two scenes, Hubbard wrote:

The correspondence between the two scenes was noted by Charles Crawford . . . who infers from it that *Locrine* copies *Selimus*. E. Koeppel . . . also notes this correspondence of scenes, but his inference is that Bullithrumble . . . is a weak copy of Strumbo. He notes also that the scene in *Selimus* is the only bit of the comic in that play.

Before seeing Koeppel's article I had arrived at the same conclusion, mainly on the ground that the comic character in *Selimus* appears only at this one place, whereas in *Locrine*, is a comic character who appears all through the earlier parts of the play, and his speech and action in the scene under consideration are consistent with his speech and action in the earlier comic scenes of the play. It is almost impossible to conceive that the author of Locrine developed the character of Strumbo from the hints given in this scene of *Selimus,* but it is perfectly natural to infer that the author of *Selimus* copied a part of one of the comic scenes of *Locrine* that suited his dramatic purpose.[20]

It may be noted first that both Koeppel and Hubbard are slightly in error in saying that the comedy in *Selimus* is restricted to this one scene. Bullithrumble reappears two scenes later (xxii), where two of his three speeches were clearly intended to be comic (lines 2074–77 and 2081–84), and he could certainly have furnished amusement, when the soldiers of Selimus would arrest him, by "stealing from them closely away" (s.d., line 2079) and then "*Exit* running away" (s.d., line 2085). Again, the amount of comedy found in each of the two plays is of little significance in determining the original form of an incident appearing in both. The tragedies of blood and conquest which *Selimus* so obviously imitates—plays like *Tamburlaine* and *Titus Andronicus*—contain only the slightest suggestion of comedy. Also Hubbard's second paragraph I find quite unconvincing. As I have observed earlier, Strumbo can hardly be said to have a consistent character of his own, but rather changes as change the situations in which he is placed; and to believe that the author of *Locrine* took freely from a comic scene in *Selimus* does not demand, as Hubbard implies, that one maintain "that the author of *Locrine* developed the character of Strumbo from hints given in this scene of *Selimus.*"

I suspect that there would be no general agreement as to the effectiveness and hence probable precedence of the different wordings in the similar passages. Strumbo says he "trembles fearing she [his wife] would set her ten commandments in my face"—meaning, obviously, scratch his face with her ten nails, as in *2 Henry VI*, I, iii, 144–45, where the duchess of Gloucester says to the queen:

> Could I come near your beauty with my nails,
> I'ld set my ten commandments in your face.

To other instances of this expression cited by *A New English Dictionary* from Heywood's *Four P's* and Dekker's *Westward Hoe,* may be added from the *Taming of a Shrew* Kate's

> Hands off, I say, and get you from this place,
> Or I will set my ten commandments in your face.

In *Selimus* Bullithrumble says he lives "in daily feare of the breach of my wiues ten-commandments." One who interprets this merely as "fear of an infraction of orders given him by his domineering wife" may feel that the wording in *Selimus* is indeed a pale and somewhat faulty echo of that in *Locrine*. Probably, however, the author of *Selimus* intended a pun: "breach" in the sense of "infraction" and also in the sense of "assault" (Webster 3a. "The Lord had made a *breach* upon Uzza, 1 Chron. xiii, 11") or *wound* (Webster 3b, "*Breach* for *breach*, eye for eye, Lev. xxiv, 20"). But so common appears to have been the identification of the ten nails as the ten commandments that the presence or absence of intent to pun is, doubtless, of little significance in determining which of the two passages was drawn from the other.

Although none of those who have discussed the relationship of the two plays seems to have thought it worthy of mention, it seems important in this connection that

the author of *Selimus* is following his source in presenting
Corcut as oppressed by hunger and seeking food from a
poor shepherd. Early under the year 1512 Richard Knolles
records that after "both the great Bassaes and the soldiers
in generall, were all solemnly sworne vnto *Selymus*, as
their onely lord and emperour," "Corcutus, whether it
were for greefe of his hope now lost, or feare of his life
. . . secretly embarked himselfe, and so returned to
MAGNESIA." And later under the following year, in a
passage frequently parallel to speeches by Corcut in the
scene under consideration, Knolles records that

> All this while *Bostanges, Selymus* his sonne in law, lying with
> a fleet of gallies vpon the coast of IONIA, had taken from *Corcutus*
> all hope of escaping by sea: so that he was faine to hide himselfe
> in a caue neere vnto the sea side not far from SMYRNA. . . .

> After he had thus a great while in feare most miserably liued
> with countrie crabs, and other like wild fruit (a poore diet for a
> man of state) and was with extreame necessitie enforced to send
> his man for reliefe to a poore sheepheards cottage thereby, he was
> by a country peasant discouerd to *Cassumes* . . . [by whom he
> was apprehended and] carried towards the tyrant his brother at
> PRVSA.[21]

To be sure, Knolles' *History*, although portions of it may
have circulated in manuscript for some years before, was
not published until 1603, and the discrepancy in the
identification of Corcut's betrayer shows that Knolles and
the author of *Selimus* followed different sources. All the
early accounts, however, tell how Corcut fled in fear, hid
himself in a cave, lived on meagre diet until, compelled
by hunger, he issued forth and was betrayed to his enemies.[22]

Although Humber in *Locrine* declares

Long haue I liued in this desart caue,
With eating hawes and miserable rootes, (lines 1724–25)

there was in none of the many accounts preceding the play
any warrant for Humber's prolonged and miserable flight.
It would have been a remarkable coincidence indeed if the
author of *Selimus*, when his plot required he introduce
Corcut in fearful flight, tortured by hunger, forced to hide
in a cave and to seek food from a shepherd, should have
at hand a play only recently written in which Humber,
in defiance of all earlier stories about him, appears in
miserable flight, tortured by hunger and forced to hide in
a cave and seek food from a countryman—in a play, withal,
in which he would find many other lines he might appropriate.

On the basis of the comic scenes alone, it would appear
to be much "more reasonable" to assume that the author
of *Selimus*, following the suggestion of his source, wrote
the scene in which Corcut and his servant beg food from
the shepherd, and that the author of the comic additions
to *Locrine* imitated that scene, even though to do so entailed prolonging Humber's life in contradiction to all
the earlier accounts.

On the other hand, the evidence seems definitely to
indicate that the borrowing from Spenser was first made by
the author of *Locrine*, from which it was appropriated by
the author of *Selimus*. We arrive, therefore, at a rather
involved sequence of borrowing which will permit only
two possible hypotheses. *Selimus* was printed in 1594; the
present form of *Locrine* can be no earlier than 1591, when
Spenser's *Complaints* appeared, perhaps no earlier than

1593 if an indebtedness to Lodge be admitted. It is
possible that the author of one of the plays, in retaliation
perhaps for what he considered thefts by the author of
the other, deliberately appropriated, before his own play
was printed, lines or a comic situation from the offending
play. Such an occurrence, however, seems rather unlikely. A
much more likely hypothesis would be that the author of
Selimus, possibly while writing that play and certainly
after reading the story of Selimus and Corcut, set about
a revision of *Locrine*. From the historical account of the
wanderings of Corcut he constructed the wholly unau-
thorized wanderings of Humber. In *Locrine* he found or
introduced many lines from Spenser, some of which, along
with lines of his own, he used again in the play temporarily
laid aside to permit this revision. He may but need not
have been the author of an earlier form of *Locrine*.

That the same author was responsible for both plays
has, indeed, been argued, though somewhat mockingly,
by Churton Collins in seeking to disprove Grosart's ascription of *Selimus* to Greene. Citing a number of verbal
parallels between the two plays and observing that the blank
verse in the two is "in scheme and rhythm simply in-
distinguishable," he declared that "the presumptions in
favour of the author of *Locrine* having been the author of
Selimus are infinitely more cogent than the arguments
adduced in favour of Greene having been the author of
Selimus: or, to put it in other words, if Greene was the
author of *Selimus*, he must have been, according to Grosart's reasoning, the author of *Locrine*." [23]

But there is, I am aware, one objection which may be
raised to my argument that two of the most obvious insertions into an older form of *Locrine* are the lines de-

picting the first meeting of Locrine with Estrild and those presenting Humber's seven years of wandering and his meeting with Strumbo. In the former scene there are, as has been noted, repeated statements that Humber died at the time of the battle, as he had in all the previous accounts. One may, therefore, ask whether a reviser would introduce lines stressing the fact that Humber had died and then immediately afterward present him still alive, wandering and seeking food. My answer would be that I believe an Elizabethan reviser might well do so. Working through the old play the reviser would first, perhaps taking a hint from Lodge's *Elstred*, have enlarged the account of the lovers' first meeting. After this insertion had been made, he decided to reproduce the comic scene from *Selimus*, the introduction of which required that he enlarge Humber's lamentation delivered in the preceding scene immediately after the battle and transfer some of it to a later spot in the play. The awkward and wholly unhistorical result of Humber's hungry wandering for seven years, he may well have failed to notice or, perhaps, have been quite indifferent to.

It is, of course, easier to demonstrate that *Locrine* underwent revision than it is to determine the date of its original composition or to identify the dramatist or dramatists concerned. Indeed, either author or reviser (if not both) seems to have sought, as it were deliberately, to make such tasks impossible by inserting throughout the play scores of lines and phrases lifted from the works of his fellow poets as well, perhaps, as from plays of his own. The result has been that, by the citation of parallel passages, momentarily convincing arguments have been presented in behalf of several of the better known dramatists of the time.

The title-page had stated that *Locrine* was "ouerseene and corrected, By *W. S.*" The implied authorship of Shakespeare, if such was the intent of the initials W. S., may have helped the printer to sell a few additional copies, but it seems not to have produced sufficient interest to lead to a demand for a second quarto. Having been rejected by Shakespeare's fellow actors when they brought his plays together in the Folio of 1623, *Locrine* was not reprinted until it appeared in the Third Shakespeare Folio of 1664. That is the earliest recorded suggestion that the "W. S." of the title-page stood for W. Shakespeare.

Few are the critics who have not utterly rejected the ascription to Shakespeare—most of them German. Tieck, indeed, translated *Locrine* into German and pronounced it a production of Shakespeare's youthful muse, revised by him in 1595; one with "a searching eye will," he declared, "recognize his genius in every part" of the play.[24] Even Schlegel, whose discussions of the apocryphal plays are remarkable principally for the tenacity with which he held to Shakespeare's authorship, doubted his hand in *Locrine*;[25] and Ulrici was "inclined to see Shakespeare's correcting and improving hand" only in the comic scenes, a view shared by Hopkinson.[26] The most remarkable recognition of Shakespeare's hand in the play is certainly that which sees him interpolating passages from Greene and Peele into an older tragedy.[27]

Almost unanimous in denying the play to Shakespeare, the English critics have shown no such agreement in a positive ascription of its authorship. Malone attributed the play to Marlowe, "whose style it appears . . . to resemble more than that of any other known dramatick author of that age."[28] He notes such undoubted similari-

ties of style as may be found in all the imitators of Marlowe and some similarities of situation: the dying speech
of Brutus is like that of Tamburlaine (although its thought
follows, as has been shown, the speech as given in *The
Mirror for Magistrates*); Guendoline's lament at her
desertion is reminiscent of Tamburlaine's lament over
Zenocrate; as Tamburlaine fell in love with his fair captive Zenocrate, so Locrine falls in love with Estrild (as
he had, of course, since the story was first told by Geoffrey
of Monmouth). Without adducing further evidence,
Samuel Hickson in 1850,[29] expressed his conviction that
Locrine was written by Christopher Marlowe.

Critics of modern times, however, have not been inclined
to consider seriously the suggestion of Marlowe's authorship. Instead they have, with varying confidence, urged
the authorship of Kyd, Greene, or Peele. Moorman, who
thought "the two plays . . . coupled together in the ridicule which Jonson meets out to Kyd in *Poetaster*" (III, i),
argued that "a comparative study of *Locrine* and *The
Spanish Tragedie* brings so many points of resemblance
to light as to make it seem probable that they are the
works of the same author." [30] Striking points of resemblance there undoubtedly are, but they again have been
generally regarded as evidence of imitation rather than of
identical authorship.

The cases for Greene and Peele have been more elaborately argued. Undoubtedly the greater weight of critical
opinion has favored the authorship of George Peele.
Fleay,[31] after slight wavering, declared *Locrine* to be
Peele's earliest attempt at tragedy, seeing in it echoes of his
work, "some Devonshire dialect" ("Peele was a Devonshire man"), and in Strumbo ridicule of Gabriel Harvey,

whom he thought caricatured in Peele's *Old Wives Tale.*
Ward thought the play more in the manner of Peele "than
that of any dramatist with whom I am acquainted; and
the exuberant tendency of its author to classicism recalls
the same writer." [32] In 1904 W. S. Gaud published an
article listing a very large number of verbal parallels between *Locrine* and the poems and plays of Peele and declared it "almost the inevitable conclusion, that Peele here
as elsewhere is simply repeating himself in his own play
Locrine." [33] Accepting Gaud's conclusion, Schelling in
1908 regarded the play as "almost unquestionably" Peele's,
and raised "the query whether it was written in good faith
and not rather [as] a take-off on the Senecan excesses of the
moment"; [34] "Locrine is Seneca popularized with such a
vengeance that we cannot but suspect so notorious a wit
as honest George of an intent in it to parody the Senecan
craze as he later parodied the extravagances of heroical
romance in *The Old Wives Tale.*" [35]

In the same year, however, Professor Tucker Brooke, in
the introduction to his *Shakespeare Apocrypha,* voted
strongly for Greene, as had J. A. Symonds [36] many years
before. "The importance, character, and success of the
comic element," wrote Tucker Brooke, "the excessive rich-
ness of mythological allusion—far greater than in any
play of Peele's and differently employed, the extreme
rarity of run-on lines, and the general appearance of over-
decoration all indicate that the author of *Locrine* is not
Peele, and that he is Peele's more humorous, but weaker
and more florid companion, Robert Greene." [37] Brooke
accepted Churton Collins' suggestion that the same author
wrote both *Locrine* and *Selimus,* but maintained that

Grosart's ascription of the latter play to Greene possessed "a greater show of probability than Mr. Collins is willing to allow"; that as "there is no contradictory evidence and [as] the internal evidence must be agreed to point in the same direction," great weight must be given to the fact that selections from *Selimus* appear in *England's Parnassus* (1600) above the name "R. Greene." [38]

Three years before, J. M. Robertson in his volume *Did Shakespeare Write Titus Andronicus?* (1905) compared that play with *Locrine*. It was Robertson's purpose, of course, largely by the study of words, to show that *Titus Andronicus* was not written by Shakespeare, and to that end he set about building up the corpus of the works of those dramatists he thought concerned in that play. On the basis of words which he declared to be favorites of theirs, he pronounced *Locrine* a play originally by Peele but recast and revised by Greene.[39]

Although I must confess to serious doubts of the trustworthiness of the method Robertson employed, it would appear that the evidence I have presented, and presented with no thought whatsoever of identifying the dramatists, leads one to a similar if not identical conclusion. I have, I believe, given good reasons to believe that the author of *Selimus* interrupted the writing of that play to introduce new material into *The Tragedy of Locrine*. If the author of *Selimus* was Robert Greene, Greene must also have been the reviser of *Locrine;* but if *Selimus* was written by an imitator of Greene, that imitator must also have revised *Locrine*. I am not prepared to offer further argument for Greene's authorship of *Selimus,* but the case made for it by Grosart and Brooke must be recognized as a strong one.

If, however, Greene was the reviser of *Locrine*, it is necessary to modify some of the statements I have tentatively made earlier. As Greene died in September 1592, he obviously could not have read Lodge's *Complaint of Elstred* in the printed text of 1593; and Lodge is known to have sailed with Cavendish in August 1591 and may not have returned to England until after Greene's death.[40] As the two men were, however, intimate friends and had, not long before Lodge sailed, collaborated on *The Looking Glass for London and England*, it is possible that Lodge had shown his friend an early draft of his *Complaint* or perhaps only sketched for him what he purposed the poem should contain. (Beyond the date of its publication there is nothing to suggest when Lodge's poem was composed.) Again it is possible, although obviously unsafe to assume, that a draft of the *Elstred* was among the papers of the novel *Euphues' Shadow*, which Lodge, shortly before he sailed, left with Greene to have published. In either case it would be easy to understand how Greene (if he was the reviser) could have based two incidents upon the poem and yet have borrowed none of its phrasing, even while boldly lifting many passages from Spenser and, to a lesser extent, from others. Although he could have reproduced the stanza form, he could hardly have borrowed the language if he had no copy of the poem at hand; and had a copy been left with him, he might well have hesitated to make verbal borrowings from a friend's poem which, still unpublished, had been entrusted to him.

But it is not of real importance to my thesis that the reviser of *Locrine* be recognized as indebted to Lodge's poem; I am not prepared to argue that Greene was the author of *Selimus* and the reviser of *Locrine*—only that the author of the former and the reviser of the latter were one and the same man.

Neither am I prepared to argue, though I think it must be recognized as a possibility, that the author of the original draft of *Locrine* may have been William Smith, the author of *Chloris*, from which in both 1593 and 1600 excerpts were published over the initials "W. S."—in the latter year in a volume in which excerpts from Shakespeare are assigned to "W. Shakespeare." An avowed disciple of Spenser, to whom he inscribed three sonnets, Smith would certainly have been familiar with the *Complaints*. He is not, however, known to have written for the theatre, and most scholars have been quite skeptical of Warburton's claim that he had once possessed a manuscript play by a Will Smithe which dealt with mythological British history. Perhaps Smith's inexperience as a playwright led the actors to engage another to render his attempt more suitable for stage production. However, although imitation and the adoption of the conventional affectations of the day are pronounced characteristics of the verse and language of both *Chloris* and *Locrine*, I have detected in the two nothing which I think urges their common authorship.[41]

Toward a solution of the question whether or not Robert Greene was the author of *Selimus* and the reviser of *Locrine*, I can offer very little, perhaps nothing of real value. Earlier in this paper I called attention to the difference in the types of stage direction found in the serious and in the comic scenes of the play—the appending of such words as *and say* (*saith, saying*) being frequent in and restricted to the comic scenes. Less extensively a similar type of stage direction is used in *Selimus*:

Enter *Acomat* . . . and his souldiers. *Acomat* must read a letter, and then renting it say (lines 1073–74)

Baiazet fals in a sownd, and being recouered say (line 1274)

Enter *Baiazet* . . . and *Aga* led by a souldier; who k[n]eeling before *Baiazet*, and holding his legs shall say (lines 1468–70)

I have found no dramatist who can be shown to have used this type of stage direction with consistency or frequency. Marlowe used it only once ("Edward kneeles, and saith," *Edward II*, line 1436), Kyd only once (*Soliman and Perseda*, lines 230–31). In the plays of Peele it is only in *King Edward I* that anything resembling this type of stage direction is to be found, the only close approximations being

Then Lluellen spieth Elinor and Mortimer, and saith thus (lines 1013–14)

and the even less similar

They all hold up their hands, and say he shall (line 730)

Neither have I been able to find this type of stage direction in any play usually ascribed to Greene except *Alphonsus King of Aragon*. In that play, however, there are some thirty instances:

Enter the *Duke of Millain* in Pilgrims apparell, and say (lines 1268–69)

Enter a souldier and say (line 1384)

Enter *Albinius* with his sworde drawne, and say (line 644)

Enter *Carinius* in his Pilgrims clothes, and say (line 1749)

Enter *Venus* with the *Muses*, and say (line 1915) [42]

The first quartos of *Selimus, Locrine,* and *Alphonsus* were all from the press of Thomas Creede and the three plays were possibly all acted by the same company, although only on the title-page of *Selimus* are the actors named. As we cannot be certain who was responsible for the similar type of stage direction in them, dramatist, copyist, or prompter, we should hardly be justified in suspecting from the similarity of the stage directions that Greene wrote the comic scenes of *Locrine* at a time somewhat close to that at which he composed *Alphonsus.* Attention may be called, however, to the very strong argument Churton Collins advanced for dating *Alphonsus* in 1591 and to his urging that in that play also there is an apparent debt to Spenser's *Complaints.*

2

THE TRUE CHRONICLE HISTORY
OF THOMAS LORD CROMWELL

AFTER BEING ENTERED upon the Stationers' Register on 11 August 1602, there was published later in that year a quarto with a title-page which in part reads as follows: "The True Chronicle Historie of the whole life and death of *Thomas* Lord *Cromwell*. As it hath beene sundrie times publikely Acted by the Right Honorable the Lord Chamberlaine his Seruants. Written by W. S." Those who recall the judgment passed upon the play by Swinburne may marvel at my temerity in asking that they devote any time to its consideration. *"Thomas Lord Cromwell,"* wrote Swinburne, "is a piece of such utterly shapeless, spiritless, bodiless, soulless, senseless, helpless, worthless rubbish, that there is no known writer of Shakespeare's age to whom it could be ascribed without the infliction of an unwarrantable insult on that writer's memory." [1] I am undeterred by Swinburne's outburst, being convinced that all students of Shakespeare will have an interest in any play, however bad they may think it, which for a century or so was accepted as by William Shakespeare. After a second edition of the play was published in 1613—again as "Written by W. S."—*Cromwell* was included in the Third and Fourth Shakespeare Folios in 1664 and 1685, was reprinted by Shakespeare's first editor, Nicholas Rowe, and was later issued separately in 1734 by R. Walker as "A Tragedy. By Shakespear." [2]

A second reason for my being undeterred by Swinburne's pronouncement is that I suspect that he has in this instance allowed his judgment to do a courtesy to his wrath and to his love of vigorous expression. One may reject Swinburne's disapproval as unwarrantably severe without joining the camp of such nineteenth-century German critics as Schlegel, who, with great confidence, declared *Thomas Lord Cromwell* to be not only unquestionably Shakespeare's but deserving to be classed among his best and maturest works.[3] What the play of *Cromwell* is, in fact, is a loosely constructed, but by no means untypical, mixture of historical fact, fiction, hearsay, and propaganda, with little or no character portrayal but with a glorification of homely virtues and, in my opinion at least, one or two most amusing bits of comedy.

The play opens with a brief scene in which three smiths, one of them Hodge, the comedian, tell of the long hours spent in study by young Thomas Cromwell, the son of their employer. After they leave for their work, Young Cromwell in soliloquy speaks of his love of learning and calls out to the smiths to cease their hammering as it interferes with his studies.[4] While he and the smiths debate whether their work is to stop, Old Cromwell enters and reprimands his son for hindering that which has made it possible for him to go like a gentleman. Thomas then distributes coin among the workers and prophesies that he will some day build a palace where their cottage stands— a palace "As fine as is King Henries house at Sheene." Aloud Old Cromwell scolds his son for his thriftless pride, but in an aside advises the audience of his own joy and confidence in him. Left alone, Young Cromwell promises that his mounting spirit will not be held down by his low birth: Wolsey, than whom none is greater, was of no higher birth, a butcher's son. Old Cromwell now returns, followed by a Master Bowser, for whom Thomas had prepared a petition. Master Bowser, stating that he·has been commissioned to select a secretary for the English merchants at Antwerp, offers the position to Cromwell, who quickly accepts. (The elation of his simple father at Thomas's advancement is both touching and amusing.)

However much these opening scenes distort history—and that Heaven knows they do—they do not suggest composition by an unskilled dramatist. Cromwell's mounting spirit, his industrious application to study, his confidence in himself, shared by his father and by Master Bowser, assures us that we are to witness the story of a truly Renaissance figure. And in departing from history the playwright has gained simple yet effective sentiment and provided a motivation, a cause and effect, for the later events to be presented from Cromwell's career. Thomas Cromwell's father, alas, seems to have had nothing at all in common with the industrious, simple-hearted, and devoted father of the play. The modern historian informs us that the elder Cromwell was, indeed, a very rascal who was fined fifty times for selling untested beer and finally convicted of forging a document intended to prove that he held certain lands by freehold instead of by copyhold.[5] We are told further that it was the enmity between father and son which persuaded Thomas Cromwell to leave home at an early age.[6] Of his father, to be sure, the dramatist perhaps did not know, for the early historians tell little or nothing of the elder Cromwell. Cromwell himself is said never to have mentioned his father. But the dramatist in this second scene makes good use of him for both comedy and sentiment, just as later, in defiance of history, he is to present a scene in which the old man calls upon his son the Lord Chancellor, and just as, still later, Lord Cromwell's young son, Harry Cromwell, is brought in to say farewell as his father is led to execution. Lord Cromwell had but one son; he was then twenty-seven and had already been summoned to Parliament as a peer of the realm; and his name was not Harry, as in the play, but Gregory.

According to the early historians, including Foxe, whose *Acts and Monuments* seems to have been the principal source of the play, it was after rather extensive travel on the continent that Cromwell, happening to be in Antwerp, was named secretary to the English merchants. There was no Master Bowser. But as the dramatist is to present later in the play episodes from Cromwell's travels, and is to omit such intervening incidents as Cromwell's service as a soldier and his embassage to the Pope in behalf of the city of Boston, he quite wisely introduces Bowser, who both motivates Cromwell's leaving home for the continent and reappears to serve as a link between the two plots of the play.

The sub-plot, which is introduced in the next scene, scene iii, is skilfully woven into the story of the main plot, for each figure in the sub-plot has some individual contact with Cromwell himself and moves, at approximately the same time, from England to the continent and then back to England. Scene iii opens with a soliloquy by Bagot, a broker—a soliloquy in which he reports that he has caused his old master's son, Banister, to be arrested

for a debt owed to the Florentine merchant Fryskiball.
Fryskiball had, however, not been previously advised of
the action Bagot had taken, and when upon entering he
learns of it, he explains that he purposely had not called
on Banister for payment, knowing him to be already hard
pressed by other creditors. Bagot insists that Banister is a
prodigal deserving no pity. Banister and his wife, brought
in by the arresting officers, convince Fryskiball that Bagot
had acted from envy and hatred. The Italian accordingly
dismisses the officers and, promising he will never press
them for the debt, invites Banister and his wife to dinner.
He will, he says, within three days return to his native
Florence. (There, of course, we are to encounter him
again midway in the play.) Bagot remains on stage to
close the scene as he had begun it—with a soliloquy in
which he voices his hatred of Banister and his plan to buy
up Banister's debts, as though in good will but in truth
to make his plague greater.

Although in the early quartos the play is divided into
neither acts nor scenes, it is usual, and I have no doubt
correct, to indicate the close of Act I at this point. The
principal character or characters of both plots have been
introduced and their true natures rather well suggested.
The setting of both plots has been England, Putney for
the story of Cromwell, London for that of the Banisters,
Bagot, and Fryskiball. We have been advised of Cromwell's removal to Antwerp and of Fryskiball's plan to
return to Florence. Further indication that Act I closes
here is the introduction at this point of a chorus to advise
us that Cromwell is now ledger to the English merchants
at Antwerp; that Bannister, to escape Bagot's hate, has with
his wife and children fled to the same city; and that thither

Bagot has pursued him, having sent before his bills of debt. Throughout the next three scenes, which we may presume to be Act II, the setting remains Antwerp and the two plots develop together or, perhaps we may say, merge into one.

In scene i of Act II Cromwell in soliloquy notes his discontent with his present work; his greatest wish is to travel. Mistress Banister enters to ask his aid in behalf of her husband, who on Bagot's complaint is held by the governor. Cromwell promises what aid he can give.

In scene ii after telling, again in soliloquy, of his determination that the Banisters be destroyed, Bagot says that he has brought with him from England jewels which he should sell in Antwerp for £5000 but which, because they could not be easily sold in England, he had got for a mere £300. Cromwell, entering, urges Bagot to show kindness to Banister, but the broker interprets this concern as hypocrisy, and when Cromwell insists that it is not, Bagot declares that, because of the position he holds,

> . . . if your conscience were as white as Snow,
> It will be thought that you are other wise.

Cromwell at once decides that he will surrender his position; he will not remain another two hours in Antwerp; his books are in order; he will visit Italy.

Hodge, one of the smiths who had appeared in scene i, now reappears and tells of the horrors of the Channel crossing in a narrative soliloquy which in the mouth of a skillful comedian might be very amusing. He quickly accepts Cromwell's suggestion that he accompany him to Italy.

Scene iii of Act II presents the Governor of the English

House, Bagot, and the Banisters. The governor wishes
Cromwell good fortune on his travels but laments that

> We hardly shall finde such a one as he
> To fit our turnes; his dealings were so honest.

Having offered within £200 of Bagot's price for the jewels,
the governor now offers to split the difference if Bagot
will release Banister, but Bagot replies:

> To do him good I will not bate a penie.

Scarcely has Mistress Banister prayed God "To let his
heauy wrath fall on [Bagot's] head," before there enters
Master Bowser, who, it will be remembered, had been
responsible for Cromwell's appointment in Antwerp. He
reports to the governor that the English king's treasury
had recently been robbed of its choicest jewels; that the
thief, before being hanged, had confessed to selling them to
Bagot, who is reported to be in Antwerp and whom he,
Bowser, has been sent to return to England. After Bagot
has been seized and carried off, Bowser reports that Bagot's
goods, valued at £5000, the king had given to the Antwerp merchants, and that they in turn present them to
Banister, one of their company who had met misfortune.
As at the end of Act I—and as so often in the drama—all
on stage go in to dinner.

Although there is not, as there was at the end of Act I,
a chorus to indicate it, modern editors are clearly correct
in marking this the end of Act II. As in Act I a unity of
place has been strictly observed. By means which seem not
the least improbable, all the characters who appeared in
both plots in Act I have been transported to Antwerp and
there brought together, with the exception of Old Cromwell and his two nameless workmen and, of course, Fryski-

ball, the Florentine merchant who had aided Banister and whose meeting with Cromwell is reserved for the following act. The action of each scene develops naturally, if not inevitably, out of that of the preceding scenes. Whatever opinion one may have of the playwright as a poet, one can hardly deny that, having accepted the material he has chosen, the author has plotted his first two acts with a skill approaching mastery.

And the same technical skill is apparent in the first two scenes of Act III. In scene i Cromwell and Hodge enter "in their shirtes, and without Hattes," having just been robbed by banditti. They set up bills explaining their misfortune and asking aid. Fryskiball enters and, recognizing them as Englishmen, gives them what money his purse contains and offers more if they will accompany him to his house. But Cromwell explains that what he has given is sufficient to get them to Bononia, whither he must hasten in an effort to save the life of the Earl of Bedford, whom the French king has sold unto his death.

In this scene the author has taken considerable liberty with the facts of this story as originally told by Bandello and repeated by Foxe, but it seems clear that he not only knew what he was doing but had sufficient reason for his alterations. In the earlier accounts Cromwell's meeting with Fryskiball was said to have taken place on a visit to Italy several years prior to his assuming the position with the English merchants at Antwerp, when, as a follower in a defeated French invasion, he found himself penniless in Florence; Fryskiball not only succored him but gave him a position in his house, where he remained for several years. The dramatist, having decided to omit the undramatic incident of Cromwell's serving with the French in an ill-fated invasion of Italy, accordingly substitutes the banditti as the cause of Cromwell's misfortune. Again, rather than make necessary two trips by Cromwell to Italy, one of which would seriously retard the development of the Banister-Bagot plot, the dramatist wisely sent him from Putney straight to Antwerp. Obvious, of course, are the reasons for not permitting Cromwell to accept the tendered hospitality of Fryskiball. He must hasten to rescue Bedford in Bononia, whither we may assume he was on his way when he encountered the banditti. The two widely separated incidents are thus skilfully combined.

The device by which Cromwell rescues the Earl of Bedford in the following scene is admittedly unconvincing; but it is a device similar to that in several Elizabethan plays and has been traced to the widely read romance by Heliodorus, *The Aethiopian History*. Foxe had merely recorded that Bedford reported to King Henry how Cromwell "by his singular device and policy . . . had done for him at Bologna, being there in the King's affairs in extreme peril." Drayton in his *Legend of Great Cromwell*, written later than the play, has Cromwell dismiss the rescue in a single line:

RUSSELL, whose Life (some said) that I had sav'd . . .
(line 457)

But however unconvincing the rescue in the play, however much it may suggest romance, it is nonetheless characteristic of much of Elizabethan drama, and it provides an opportunity for some most amusing comedy.

To the earl, whose inn is surrounded by those intent on taking him prisoner and sending his body unto France, a servant brings word that entrance is craved by a Neapolitan who has persuaded the besiegers that without shedding a drop of blood he will deliver Bedford to them. Disguised as a Neapolitan, Cromwell, entering with Hodge, reveals himself to the earl and explains that since the Mantuans are at deadly strife with the Bononians, the earl and he will be safe if they can by policy reach the Mantuan port. He orders Hodge to change suits with the earl and, the exchange completed, he and Bedford hurry on to Mantua after announcing to the besiegers that the one they seek is ready to surrender. With the change in clothes, Hodge at once feels honor creeping on. "My Nobilitie is wonderfull melancholie," he says. "Is it not most Gentleman like to be melancholie?" And when the Bononians draw aside the curtain and stand watching him, Hodge is writing a letter.

"Fellow William," he writes, "I am not as I haue beene: I went from you a Smith, I write to you as a Lord. . . . I do commend my Lordship to Raphe & to Roger, to Bridget & to Doritie, & so to all the youth of Putnay."

"Sure," says the governor of Bononia,

> Sure, these are the names of English Noblemen,
> Some of his speciall friends, to whom he writes:
> But stay, he doth adresse himselfe to sing.

The song is not printed, but, if the commedian taking the part of Hodge was good, there can be no doubt that the scene was highly amusing. A messenger now arrives from Mantua announcing that the earl has reached that city safely and threatening the Bononians that Mantua will withdraw the truce between them unless Hodge is released.

To this point the play has, as I think we must agree, been exceptionally well plotted. Each scene has developed naturally out of the preceding scene. Incidents in Cromwell's career, true or fictitious, have been selected or created, and other incidents changed or omitted, in order to obtain three distinct periods in three definite places. Further, by the overlapping of characters, the two plots have been more closely knit together than is the case in the great majority of Elizabethan plays. This first half of the play certainly does not deserve all of the strong adjectives in which Swinburne condemned the play as a whole. "Utterly shapeless, . . . bodiless, . . . senseless, helpless" this first half certainly is not. Whatever verdict one may pass on the verse in them, I think it evident that these eight scenes are from the pen of an experienced and skillful playmaker.

But just at this point, at the end of Act III, scene ii, everything seems to collapse. From now on the action is pathetically episodic; the play becomes, indeed, shapeless, bodiless, helpless, although the material with which the later scenes are concerned furnished infinitely more dramatic situations. And this sudden change in dramatic skill is signalled by a chorus appended to the scene I have just discussed—a chorus which provokes no little bewilderment:

> Thus farre you see how *Cromwelles* fortune passed.
> The Earle of *Bedford*, being safe in *Mantua*,
> Desires *Cromwells* companie into France,
> To make requitall for his courtesie:
> But *Cromwell* doth denie the Earle his sute,
> And telles him that those partes he meant to see,
> He had not yet set footing on the land,
> And so directlie takes his way to Spaine:
> The Earle to France, and so they both do part.

There needs no chorus come from the wings to tell us that Bedford has arrived safely in Mantua. The messenger from Mantua had proclaimed the earl's safe arrival just twenty lines before. But it takes more than a chorus to make us understand why Bedford should directly take his way to France when in the preceding scene it was the allies of the French king who were seeking to take him prisoner and send him into France. In one of the few passages of bombast, Bedford had there cried:

> First shall the Ocean be as drie as sand,
> Before aliue they send me vnto *France*.
> Ile haue my bodie first bored like a Siue,
> And die as *Hector*, gainst the *Mirmidons*,
> Eare *France* shall boast *Bedfordes* their prisoner . . .

Whether he was forgetful of or undaunted by his narrow escape, Bedford's sudden decision to go at once to France is a matter of no importance to the audience of this play, for when we next see Bedford he is in England, and no mention is then made of his having returned to France. Neither is there any reason why we should here be told that Cromwell now goes on to Spain, since the chorus continues:

> Now let your thoughtes, as swift as is the winde,
> Skip some few yeares, that *Cromwell* spent in trauell,
> And now imagine him to be in England,
> Seruant vnto the maister of the Roules . . .

The only explanation of why the writer of this chorus thought it necessary to refer to Bedford's going into France and to Cromwell's going to Spain would seem to be that he had only the rudest knowledge of what constituted material for a play; that, faced by the voluminous account in his sources, he was haunted by the fear that nothing should be omitted without mention. This same concept of the province of the chronicle play is to be observed in a later chorus, as I shall note. But certainly it is not the concept of the plotter of the first half of the play. He, as I have tried to show, was capable of constructing a closely knit plot, and in order to do so, had no hesitation in either changing the incidents recorded in his sources or omitting them altogether.

From now on the play becomes hopelessly episodic—especially in the following six scenes. The setting of the next scene, as the chorus had suggested it would be, is the house of the Master of the Rolls, Sir Christopher Hales, who has prepared a banquet to honor Cardinal Wolsey. Cromwell, even before he speaks, attracts the attention of Wolsey and is praised by Hales as a traveler and linguist. Questioned by Wolsey, Cromwell praises England at the expense of France, Italy, Spain, Germany, and Holland, and is at once by Wolsey created "Solliciter of our causes" and promised "Shortlie his fortune shall be lifted higher." Wolsey departs, taking Cromwell with him.

And now, after an absence of only one scene, the chorus reappears. Many years we learn have elapsed:

> Now *Cromwells* highest fortunes doth begin,
> *Wolsay*, that loued him as he did his life,
> Committed all his treasure to his hands.
> *Wolsay* is dead, and *Gardiner*, his man,
> Is now created Bishop of *Winchester:*
> Pardon if we omit all *Wolsayes* life,
> Because our play dependes on *Cromwelles* death.
> Now sit and see his highest state of all;
> His haight of rysing and his sodaine fall.

Amusingly naive is the apology for omitting "all Wol-
sayes life," yet it seems strange that, having gone to the
trouble of introducing Wolsey at all, the dramatist should
have thought a sole appearance sufficient for one who was a
most stage-worthy figure as well as the greatest single
influence on the career of Thomas Cromwell. One may
well ask whether, like so many of the chronicle plays of
the time, *The True Chronicle History of the whole life
and death of Thomas Lord Cromwell* had not originally
been in two parts—two full-length plays which were later
reduced into the text which has survived. Such a supposition may be supported by the three irregular appearances
of the chorus, two of which, separated by a single scene
of 108 lines, serve merely to acquaint us with the information not given in the play proper—information, moreover,
which is of very slight significance when compared to other
information not presented in the play and yet not mentioned in the choruses.

As the last chorus asks the audience to

> . . . sit and see his highest state of all;
> His haight of rysing and his sodaine fall,

it seems strange indeed that no mention is made in the
play of the highest offices held by Lord Cromwell, although these are noted by Foxe and others. Foxe had
written that in 1537 Cromwell "was made knight of the
garter, and not long after was advanced to the earldom
of Essex, and made great chamberlain of England: over
and besides all which honours, he was constituted also
vice-regent to the king, representing his person; which
office, although it standeth well by the law, yet seldom
hath there been seen any besides this Cromwell . . ." [7]

And in his *Legend of Great Cromwell* Drayton later was to have Cromwell list the honors he had received from the king:

> For first from Knighthood rising in degree,
> The Office of the Jewell-house my lot,
> After, the Rolles he frankly gave to Me,
> From whence a Privie Counseller I got,
> Then of the Garter: and then Earle to be
> Of *Essex:* yet sufficient these were not,
>> But to the great Viceregencie I grew,
>> Being a Title as Supreme as new.[8]

None of these last three honors is mentioned in the play. If the play was either composed or revised in years immediately prior to its publication in 1602, it is possible that the dramatist may well have thought it the better part of valor to omit anything which might be construed as intended to bring to mind the fall of another Earl of Essex, Robert Devereux. Similarly he may have thought it inexpedient to introduce any reference to Anne of Cleves (d. 1557), who is not mentioned in the play, even though the marriage he arranged between the king and her well shows the influence Cromwell exerted, and even though Foxe made clear that it was Henry's determination to free himself of her that brought Cromwell's fall. But it is strange indeed that no mention is made in the play of the vice-regency, that "Title as Supreme as new," the inclusion of which would emphasize, as the more modest titles given him in the play do not, Cromwell's fall from the "highest state of all."

But I have perhaps got too far ahead of my summary of the play. Two acts remain. In the first scene of Act IV the dukes of Norfolk and Suffolk request in the king's name certain writings which Wolsey had left in Cromwell's keeping. After the dukes have departed with the documents, Bedford enters—"hastily" a stage direction notes, welcomes Cromwell back to England and, promising to commend him to the king, departs with equal haste, having been on the stage for only nine lines. Suffolk returns to greet Cromwell as "Sir Thomas." Two lines later Norfolk enters to announce that Cromwell has been made Master of the Jewel House, Chief Secretary to the king, a member of the Privy Council. Norfolk has scarcely ended his five line speech before Bedford returns to report that Cromwell has now been made Lord Keeper of the Privy Seal and Master of the Rolls. All save Gardiner leave to escort the new Councillor to the king, but Gardiner remains to express his envy and his determination that Cromwell's glory shall be dimmed.

As doubtless one may find in the chronicle plays of the period other instances in which the telescoping of history requires that honors come to one at such a furious pace, I shall not urge that such telescoping here argues revision. But it is strange that immediately following the implication of the chorus that Cromwell has been back in England for a number of years, the Earl of Bedford should cry out upon meting him:

> How now, whose this?
> *Cromwell*, by my soule! welcome to England:
> Thou once didst saue my life, didst not *Cromwell?*
>
> (IV, i, 30–32)

In the text as it now stands only one scene separates this speech from Cromwell's rescue of the earl. Would it be too fanciful to suggest that the last line of Bedford's greeting,

> Thou once didst save my life, didst not *Cromwell?*

is just the sort of allusion we might expect to find in Part II of a play to refresh the audience's recollection of an incident which had appeared in Part I?

In the next scene characters from the sub-plot reappear and several incidents are introduced for the purpose of showing that the high honors which had come to him had not caused Cromwell to forget his early friends. Fryskiball enters, now "very poor," and in soliloquy relates how his fortune has been lost at sea and he, as a result, is despised by those who owe him money and kindness. Old Seely and his wife, who had, they say, befriended Cromwell in his youth and now need help, set themselves to await his entry. Cromwell enters, "the Mace caryed before him," with Norfolk, Suffolk, and attendants. He at once recognizes the old couple, acknowledges his debt to them, and rewards them handsomely. He likewise recognizes Fryskiball from afar off and sends a messenger to command the Florentine's presence at his house. Then appears the stage direction *"Enter Old* Cromwell *like a Farmer";* and Cromwell, setting state aside, kneels before his aged father. All leave save Fryskiball. Banister and his wife, entering, at once rush to embrace their sometime benefactor; now wealthy, they are happy to repay him. They leave for Cromwell's house. But warning that less happy days lie ahead is sounded earlier in the scene when Gardiner, as Cromwell bestows his gifts, remarks in an aside to Norfolk:

> . . . see you this same bubble,
> That same puffe? But marke the end, my Lord,
> Marke the ende.

In the brief scene which follows, scene iii of Act IV, two merchants on their way to pay large sums to Banister, tell of a jest of Lord Cromwell's at the expense of Bishop Gardiner—a jest not originally attributed to Cromwell. This is followed by a scene at Cromwell's house where the dukes of Norfolk and Suffolk, along with Old Cromwell, Fryskiball and Seely, have been invited to dinner. Cromwell speaks of his debts to the last three, and offers thanks with handsome gifts.

Neither of the two last mentioned scenes advances the plot to any real extent. Cromwell's wit is evidenced in other parts of the play and the ill feeling between Gardiner and Cromwell is too often stressed to require telling of the jest. So too, the dinner at Cromwell's, though it serves to elaborate his thankfulness to Fryskiball, for the most part merely underscores the gratitude and lack of worldly pride shown in Cromwell's earlier meeting with his three benefactors. The inclusion of these two scenes suggests a more leisurely telling of the story than is observable elsewhere in the latter half of the play.

In Act IV, scene v, two scoundrels whose forfeited lives have been spared by Bishop Gardiner on the promise that they will risk their lives for him, are told that they must swear that they had heard Cromwell wish a dagger in King Henry's heart. Assuring them that bearing such testimony would be a worthy deed, Gardiner orders them to kneel and absolves them by placing a crucifix upon their heads and sprinkling holy water on their brows. He will avenge the church, he says, on him who had pulled down the abbeys and changed religion. When Norfolk, Suffolk, and Bedford enter, the false witnesses testify as instructed. Bedford abruptly leaves. The others accepting the report, Gardiner explains that though they could

never convict Cromwell in a public trial, the king having
faith in none but Cromwell, they can trap him by an act
which Cromwell had himself persuaded the king to sign,
an act providing that any councillor convicted of high treason be executed without public trial. They will "pres-
ently to Lambeth," where Cromwell will come from the
court that night, and there arrest him.

Modern editors of the play at this point begin Act V, a
division which overlooks the fact that the action of the
next scene follows immediately upon, if indeed it does not
overlap, the action in the preceding. Bedford, who in the
earlier scene had abruptly left after hearing the false
witnesses, is seeking Cromwell in the hope that, by warning
him not to go to Lambeth, he may thwart Gardiner's
malice. Cromwell enters with his train, but he asks Bedford's pardon for not stopping to talk; he has been "sent
for to the king." Four lines later Cromwell, having so
quickly completed his visit with the king, returns with
train; but again his haste is such he cannot stop:

> Lord *Marques Dorset* beeing sicke to death,
> I must receaue of him the priuie seale:

at Lambeth they may talk their fill. Bedford hastily writes
Cromwell a note of warning which he sends after him by
messenger.

In the next scene, as he is taking a barge to Lambeth,
Cromwell receives Bedford's letter, but he puts it unread
into his pocket, though the messenger, as he had been
instructed, urges him to read it at once since it concerns him
near.

Here, I feel, the dramatist has succeeded in building a
real suspense—and he has done so by ignoring, changing,

and supplementing history. In keeping with his wish to
portray Gardiner as a vicious schemer, the dramatist has
attributed to his malice—and in an entirely different context—the testimony that Cromwell had wished a dagger
in the king. In Foxe the report was that "touching the
king's divorce with the lady Anne of Cleves, [Cromwell]
had said these words: 'That he wished his dagger in him
that had dissolved or broken that marriage'; hereupon it
was objected against him by Thomas duke of Norfolk, and
others, that it was spoken against the king, who, at that
time being in love with Catherine Howard, was the chief
cause and author of that divorce." [9] Gardiner's name is
not mentioned in this connection at all. Neither is there any
recorded historical basis for the unsuccessful efforts of
Bedford to warn his friend not to go to Lambeth. The
situation is strongly reminiscent of the efforts to warn
Julius Caesar of what to expect on the Ides of March,
and may well have been suggested by Shakespeare's
tragedy.

In scene iii Gardiner and the nobles, with "Sargiant at
armes, the Harauld, and halberts," await Cromwell's
coming at Lambeth. On his arrival the herald proclaims
him traitor and the sergeant arrests him in King Henry's
name. At Gardiner's order he is taken to the Tower. Bedford alone shows sympathy.

In scene iv, both to delay and to emphasize the tragedy,
two nameless citizens marvel at the suddenness of Cromwell's fall:

> He that in court secure will keepe himselfe,
> Must not be great, for then he is enuied at,
> The Shrub is safe, when as the Cedar shakes.

In the final scene of the play, Cromwell, in the Tower, recalls how honors had come to him unsought and unlooked for (though in Act I he had stated his ambition "to flourish and controule"); then at long last he remembers and, too late, reads the warning Bedford had sent him. The nobles entering, Gardiner reports that the king, advertised of Cromwell's guilt, will by no means admit him to his presence. After Gardiner has refused to deliver a letter to the king, Sir Ralph Sadler agrees to do so and leaves with it. Gardiner orders that Cromwell be executed at once, though his departure is delayed to permit him to take his farewell of his son, who receives ten lines of advice and a reminder that Gardiner is the cause of his father's fall. After he has embraced Bedford, Cromwell is led off, and four lines later his severed head is brought in just as Sir Ralph Sadler returns with a reprieve and an order that Cromwell be brought at once to the king. Too late Gardiner, his conscience awakened, wishes that Cromwell were alive again; and Norfolk closes the play with:

> Come, let vs to the King, whom well I know,
> Will grieue for *Cromwell* that his death was so.

Here again, the dramatist shows his unwillingness to be bound by his historical material. None can object to his reducing the length of Cromwell's imprisonment from many months to a single night, and Foxe, who had idealized Cromwell almost to the extent that the dramatist does, is authority for Norfolk's closing couplet—that the king did "shortly after, lament his death, wishing to have his Cromwell alive again." No mention is made, of course, of what Foxe, Drayton, and others recognize as the chief reason for Cromwell's fall: Henry's wish to repudiate

Lady Anne of Cleves that he might be free to marry Catherine Howard, "which otherwise it is to be thought," wrote Foxe, "during the life of Cromwell could not so well be brought to pass." [10] The king is represented as only indirectly responsible for Cromwell's fall—as certain, indeed, to have come to his aid had only he been correctly informed.

The failure of the king himself to appear in the play is, of course, no indication that the play has been in any way tampered with, for we should hardly expect him to be brought upon the stage during the reign of his daughter. The dramatists had yet to assume the boldness and impudence found in some of the plays written during the reign of King James. Yet I have, I think, shown reason to believe (1) that the technical skill shown in Act IV and the last scene of Act III is far inferior to that possessed by the author of the first half of the play; (2) that different parts of the play reveal contradictory concepts of the nature and province of the chronicle play; and (3) that the difference in skill and concept, supported by the episodic structure and the strange omissions in much of the second half of the play, as well as by the erratic introduction of the choruses and the irrelevant information they recite, suggest that *Thomas Lord Cromwell* is not the work of a single author. Possibly the play, begun by one dramatist, was completed by another; possibly it is the product of collaboration by writers of unequal ability; possibly the text we have is that of a version which has been constructed by telescoping two plays into one.

I find some unconscious support for this view in a remark by the late Tucker Brooke. In his brief comment on the play in his volume *The Shakespeare Apocrypha,* Mr.

Brooke observed that "The scenes of *Cromwell* are disconnected and undramatic to such a degree that the real plot cannot be said to begin before the close of the third Act." [11] Obviously he recognized what I have been trying to demonstrate: that the play seems to divide itself into two imperfectly related parts. Mr. Brooke suggested as a point of division the end of Act III. From the analysis of the play I have given, I think it more reasonable to set the end of Act III, scene ii, as the point of division. Neither would I accept Mr. Brooke's suggestion that this imperfect relationship is attributable to the scenes throughout being too disconnected and undramatic. It is, as I think I have shown, only the scenes after Act III, scene ii, after the rescue of Bedford, that are notably episodic. To that point the scenes are carefully connected and seem no more episodic than all scenes must be in a dramatic presentation of a period of time much greater than that required for actual performance. Indeed, I can think of no history play of the period—those of Shakespeare included—in which the scenes are by anticipatory statements so consciously knit together as are those of the first half of *Cromwell*.

I regret that I cannot lay claim to an ear sufficiently sensitive to enable me to speak with some confidence of whether or not two or more hands are to be recognized in the verse of the play. The verse throughout seems equally uninspired, the occasional rime equally forced. That often somewhat tedious adornment of Elizabethan drama, the aphorism, is scattered throughout the entire play, and a fondness for classical allusions is to be noted only twice— oddly enough in the mouth of the comic Hodge, as he relates the horrors of his Channel crossing, and in that of the besieged Earl of Bedford in his inn at Bononia.

It is, of course, quite possible that the "Written by W. S." of the title-page truthfully declared *Thomas Lord Cromwell* written by a dramatist whose initials happened to be the same as those of William Shakespeare. We know that there were at the time one or two dramatists other than Shakespeare with those initials; and we know further that one of them wrote at least one play for the Lord Chamberlain's Men, the company of actors with whom Shakespeare was connected and by whom the title-page states *Cromwell* had been acted.[12] If, however, it be assumed that the initials were placed on the title-page with fraudulent intent, it follows that they are of no value in restricting from consideration as possible authors those whose initials were not W. S. Accordingly, some one hundred and more years ago Richard Farmer suggested the authorship of Thomas Heywood, perhaps the most prolific and certainly not the least gifted dramatist of the time. In 1891 A. F. Hopkinson suggested Robert Greene's authorship and, alone among English critics, recognized the revising hand of William Shakespeare.[13] Neither nomination seems to have been seconded. More worthy of consideration perhaps is the more fully argued suggestion of Frederick G. Fleay, whose guesses, if at times fanciful, were always ingenious and reflected his wide knowledge of the literature of the time. Fleay assigned *Cromwell* to the poet Michael Drayton. The principal reason for his ascription was, apparently, his wish to discover some works by Drayton which might be assigned to years in which Drayton seemed strangely inactive. Possibly Fleay was also influenced in his ascription by the fact that some few years after the printing of the play Drayton was to use much of the same material in his *Legend of Great Cromwell*.

Oddly enough, however, the argument which Fleay advanced for Drayton's authorship of the play furnishes almost convincing proof that the play was not written by Drayton—at least not during the years of the literary inactivity which was Fleay's reason for assigning the play to him.

According to Fleay, and I think him quite correct: "Drayton, habitually, when offended with any writer or patron, ceased to mention him, and more than that, cut out of his later editions any mention that existed in earlier ones. In this way he cancelled his compliments to the Bedfords in his *Mortimeriados* and his *Sonnets* addressed to various persons." [14] Fleay notes that Drayton had dedicated works to Lucy, Countess of Bedford, in 1594, in 1595, and twice in 1596; and had in 1597 dedicated *England's Heroical Epistles* to the Countess and Earl of Bedford. In the 1600 edition of Drayton's sonnets that to the Countess of Bedford is retained, but it was withdrawn in the edition of 1602, in which year were reprinted the *Heroical Epistles* and the rewritten *Mortimeriados*, dedicated to Sir W. Aston, with no mention whatsoever of either Bedford. Accordingly Fleay dates the rupture between Drayton and his early patrons in 1601.

Fleay continues: "Examination of Henslow's list shows that, of the twenty-four plays there given [in which Drayton had some share], eighteen were written in about a year, in 1598; while in the remaining four years, 1599–1603, during which Drayton continued to write for the stage, he only assisted in producing six plays for Henslow. It seems probable that he must have been writing also for another company; he had to live, had lost his patronage from the Bedford family, and certainly produced nothing for the press. Is there any trace left of what he produced for the theatre?" [15] Answering this question in the affirimative, Fleay assigned to Drayton, along with other plays, both *Cromwell* and *The London Prodigal,* which was printed as by William Shakespeare in 1605. And then Fleay closes his discussion with the remarkable suggestion that since "The plays concerned exactly fill up the blank periods of his theatrical career," Drayton was employed as a journeyman by Shakespeare and, unwilling to have his own name used, was permitted to use W. S. or William Shakespeare.[16]

Although Fleay can never be charged with a lack of imagination, he can in this instance be convicted of a failure to re-examine the play before so glibly disposing of it. Had he reread *Cromwell* after concocting his theory, Fleay could not have failed to notice that one of its most patent features, and one distinguishing it from other versions of the life of Thomas Cromwell, is the prominence assigned to John Russell, the first earl of Bedford and the great-grandfather of Drayton's patron, Edward Russell, the third earl. Not only is Bedford the one honest and generous nobleman in the play, not only is stressed his military prowess which "made the French stirre when they hard [his] name," but, unless some barb of unsuspected irony is to be recognized, even more gratifying to the later Russells would be such a line as

A *Russell* yet was never found ingrate. (IV, i, 39)

If written by Michael Drayton, *Cromwell* would, according to Fleay's own argument, have to be dated prior to his break with the Bedfords and so prior to much of the hiatus Fleay was attempting to fill.

But there are other reasons for denying the authorship
of *Cromwell* to Drayton. Not only are many of the same
incidents, some of which I have mentioned, narrated
quite differently in the play and in the *Legend,* but the two
works present sharply differing portraits of Thomas Cromwell. To the dramatist, obviously a militant Protestant,
Cromwell was the embodiment of all the virtues, and his
death an example of virtue undermined by greed and
blind fanaticism. The idealization of Cromwell apparent
in Foxe was, as I have noted, carried even farther in the
play. To Drayton, however, Cromwell is no such paragon.
Rather he is presented as one whose fall, resulting from
his thirst for power, was not undeserved. He is made to
admit that as a minister of the English king he was retained
in the pay of foreign states, and he confesses:

> Those Lawes I made my selfe alone to please,
> To give me power more freely to my Will,
> Even to my Equals hurtfull sundrie wayes,
> (Forced to things that most doe say were ill)
> Upon me now as violently seyze,
> By which I lastly perisht by my Skill,
>   On mine owne Necke returning (as my due)
>   That heavie Yoke wherein by me they drew.
>   (lines 913–20)

It seems improbable that Drayton's view of Thomas Cromwell could have changed so radically as to permit his
authorship of both the play and the legend.

The elaborate and detailed history of the play of *Cromwell* as concocted by Arthur Acheson, it is equally difficult
either to accept or to disprove. Indeed the participation of at
least some of the authors whom he recognized seems not im-

possible and certainly less improbable than the ascription of the play to Greene or Drayton or Shakespeare. Acheson declared the original play of *Cromwell* to have been written by George Chapman and Anthony Munday in 1582–83—the "antiCatholic spirit . . . intended to cater to the public interest excited by the recent Jesuit trials and executions." [17] Originally a Pembroke play, Acheson conjectured, it about 1591 passed into the hands of Burbage, who employed that "dresser of plays," Thomas Dekker, to make a revision, his hand being "plainly recognizable in the choruses, as well as in the comic passages in which Hodge appears, where Munday's hand is overwritten." [18] This revision, Acheson further conjectured, Burbage some years later, about 1601, sold to Henslowe, who turned it over to four of his writers, Chettle, Munday, Drayton, and Wentworth Smith, in order that they might incorporate into their own lost play *The Life and Death of Cardinal Wolsey* those scenes in *Cromwell* which bore upon the career of Wolsey; [19] what was left of the Dekker revision of the Chapman-Munday play after the Wolsey material had been extracted, Henslowe surrendered to the printer. That Acheson thought our present text. *The Life and Death of Cardinal Wolsey*, he continued, must later have become the property of the King's Men for "*the Cromwell parts of 'Henry VIII' are plainly taken from the old play of 'Cromwell'* [Acheson's italics], and evidently were conveyed there through their absorption into *Wolsey* in 1601–2." [20]

Although the true history of the text of *Cromwell* may have somewhat resembled that which Acheson elaborately and ingeniously constructed, his theory obviously does not account for all that would seem to be missing in the extant

form of the play. At best it offers an explanation for there
being in *Cromwell* only the one scene dealing with that
portion of Cromwell's life which he spent as a servant of
Wolsey—a period in his life which, it should be remembered, Foxe also treats very summarily.[21] Even if it be assumed that the authors of *Cardinal Wolsey*, 1601, transferred into the play scenes from an earlier version of *Cromwell* which dealt with the relations of the two men, it must
be recognized that they could make no use of scenes concerned with Cromwell's career after the Cardinal's death.
Yet in the play, as has been noted, very sketchy indeed is
the treatment accorded the events in his later career that
illustrate either the power which he achieved or the reforms
with which the dramatist was clearly in sympathy. The
dissolution of the abbeys is referred to several times, but
only in retrospect. To be sure, the dramatist may well have
judged insufficiently dramatic such things as the part which
Cromwell played in the assembly of learned men called to
determine religious matters in 1537, his causing the people
to be instructed in the Lord's Prayer and the Creed in
English, the scriptures to be read in English, and so on.
And doubtless for other reasons it is not surprising that no
mention is made of Anne of Cleves and Catherine Howard. But Foxe recounts other incidents, omitted by the
dramatist, which could be effectively staged and made to
illustrate Cromwell's wit and judgment: those concerned
with the Maid of Kent, whom he and Cranmer tried at
Paul's Cross and revealed to be not "a holy woman, and a
prophetess inspired" but "a strong and lewd imposter";
the blood of Hayles which Cromwell caused to be brought
to Paul's Cross and there proved to be the blood of a
duck; the friar who continued to wear a cowl; the ruffian

who used to go with his hair about his shoulders (an incident which interestingly turns up in *Sir Thomas More*, III, ii, with Cromwell's part there assigned to More). But there is little reason to assume that any of these incidents must once have been in a form of the play antecedent to that which has survived. For a portion of the original play's having perished, the strongest argument is still that there is in the form we have no mention of Cromwell's highest honors—the garter, the earldom of Essex, and the vice-regency. These we should most certainly expect in a tragedy in which the audience is invited to

> . . . sit and see his highest state of all;
> His haight of rysing and his sodaine fall.

Scenes in which he received his highest honors could not, however, have been utilized in *The Life and Death of Cardinal Wolsey* or any other play except one in which Cromwell himself was the central figure. If such scenes were written and then removed from the play, the only reasonable explanation of their removal would seem to be censorship or fear of censorship.

No objective evidence has ever been presented for the dating of *Cromwell*. Sir Edmund Chambers merely gives "by 1602," which was of course the year of its publication. Others, basing their opinions probably upon the naïveté of the chorus and upon the ambitious and unsatisfactory attempt to present "the whole life and death of *Thomas Lord Cromwell*," have assigned the play to the early 1590s. There would appear to be no reason why soon after 1590 one should hesitate to present or to approve for presentation a play dealing with an earlier Earl of Essex. For a few years after 1599, however, there was certainly good reason; for though there was of course no blood relationship, and though the careers of the two men were quite different, any praise of the earlier Earl of Essex might well be construed as praise of Robert Devereux, Earl of Essex, pamphlets in whose defense had been expressly forbidden in November 1599.[22]

That at least one tended, when thinking of the one earl, to call to mind the other is suggested by a letter to Sir Robert Cecil, preserved among the papers at Hatfield House. It is an unsigned and undated letter, assigned by the editors to "1599 (?)".

I did make Sir John Stanhope acquainted with certain words that Sir John Symonds did speak of your honour, and of my Lord of Essex: . . . these were the words that your honour should say to my Lord of Essex that my Lord Cromwell did lose his head for a less matter, and with that my Lord of Essex should offer to strike your honour . . .[23]

During the sixty years which had by 1599 elapsed since the execution of Cromwell, there were surely others who had lost their heads "for a less matter"; it must have been their both being earls of Essex which provoked this comparison.

As there is no apparent reason why the higher titles of Cromwell should have been omitted in a dramatization of his career prepared earlier than 1599, one may perhaps be the more inclined to recognize two possible echoes of Shakespeare which, if they be allowed, indicate that the present form of *Cromwell* dates no earlier than 1599 or 1600. Both I have previously referred to. First, there are the choruses, which, crude and awkward though they be, are nevertheless reminiscent of those of *King Henry V* in wafting the audience o'er the seas and inviting them to sit and see. Then there is the wholly unhistorical and previously unrecorded incident in which Bedford's messenger brings Cromwell the note of warning and unsuccessfully urges him to read it at once as "it doth concerne you neare," a situation which closely parallels and may perhaps have been suggested by Artemidorus' proffered and rejected schedule in *Julius Caesar*, III, i.

A date close to 1600 for *Cromwell* is also urged by its relation to both *The Book of Sir Thomas More* and to the plays on Cardinal Wolsey. The title-page of the 1602 quarto of *Cromwell* claims that the play "hath beene sundrie times . . . Acted" but offers no indication how recently it had been acted. The August 1602 entry upon the Stationers' Register declares it "lately acted." The words *hath beene* and *lately* both suggest performance in the not too distant past, but suggest also, as does the play's having found its way to the press, that it was, when entered upon the Stationers' Register in August 1602, no longer on the stage. *The Life of Cardinal Wolsey*, however, seems definitely to have been then upon the stage, for in May and June of that year Henslowe paid Henry Chettle for "mendynge" it,[24] and "on the 25 July Richard Hadsor wrote to Sir R. Cecil of the attainder of the Earl of Kildare's grandfather 'by the policy of Cardinal Wolsey, as it is set forth and played now upon the stage in London.' "[25] The "mendynge" for which Chettle received payment was certainly to his own *Life of Cardinal Wolsey*, which he wrote between June and August, 1601, and to which later he, with Munday, Drayton, and Wentworth Smith, wrote a Part I, *The Rising of Cardinal Wolsey*, between August and November 1601.[26] It so happens, therefore, that of the three plays dealing with Henry VIII's great chancellors, Wolsey, More, and Cromwell, the only one which can be definitely dated is the one which has not survived. Although the grounds on which the argument is based are obviously ambiguous and could even be used to support a contrary conclusion, there appears some reason to believe that the order in which the three were written was *More, Cromwell, Wolsey.* One may at once question such an order because of the acknowledged superiority of *More* to *Cromwell;* but as so little is known of either the authorship of *Cromwell* or the history of its text, the question of dramatic and poetic merit has little bearing on which may have been written first.

In both *More* and *Cromwell* there is attributed to the central figure a jest which in earlier tellings had been attributed to another. In III, ii, of *More* Sir Thomas encounters a ruffian who had vowed not to cut his hair for three years. Because he would not have him break his vow and

> . . . because it is an odious sight
> To see a man thus hairie,

More sentences him to three years in Newgate. The identical story had earlier been told by Foxe of Cromwell's meeting and sentencing the long-haired ruffian.[27] The episode does not appear in the play of *Cromwell*—at least not in the play we have. We must, therefore, make one of three assumptions: (1) that the writer in *More* deliberately lifted from an earlier form of the tragedy of *Lord Cromwell* an episode which was omitted when that play was revised; (2) that a jest attributed to Lord Cromwell in the tragedy's principal source was discarded by the dramatist though it was later recognized as sufficiently telling to justify unwarranted inclusion in the dramatic story of another Lord Chancellor; or (3) that one of the dramatists responsible for *More*, the earlier play, having in his reading met with a jest which he liked and thought usable, inserted it into his play without regard to its original attribution to Cromwell, and by thus rendering it less acceptable in a drama concerned with the chancellor about whom it had originally been told, suggested the substitution of the previously unrelated jest of Cromwell at the expense of Bishop Gardiner in IV, iii. I suggest, although not without hesitation, that the third is the safest assumption. If, to be sure, *More* was never acted, this would be true perhaps only if some of the same dramatists were concerned in both plays, and only if *Cromwell* was composed at a time when it still seemed reasonable that *More* might be licensed for presentation.

If it be agreed that the most likely order of the three plays was *More, Cromwell, Wolsey*, the surviving manuscript of *Sir Thomas More* would appear to furnish additional evidence for dating our play of *Cromwell* not far from 1599–1600. There has, I believe, been general agreement that the original hand in the manuscript of *More* is that of Anthony Munday and, to quote Sir Edmund Chambers, that "the changes in Munday's script put the original text [of *More*] earlier than his *Heaven of the Mynde* (1602) and later than *John a Kent*," [28] the manuscript of which bears, in another's hand, the date "—Decembris 1596"—not necessarily the date at which that play was written but presumably the date at which the surviving copy was made. If we accept for *More* a date in the late 1590s and see *Cromwell* as coming between it and the

Life of Cardinal Wolsey, written in the late summer of 1601, we again arrive at a date for *Cromwell* close to 1599–1600.

But I have argued, and I think given good reason to believe, that the play as we have it represents some form of revision or telescoping. It may, therefore, be the revision and not the original composition which should be dated after *Julius Caesar* and *Henry V* and after the difficulties of Robert Devereux, Earl of Essex. Indeed, it may well have been the difficulties of the then Earl of Essex which both suggested a revival of a play presenting the story of an earlier Essex and, quite naturally, necessitated the extensive deletions which characterize our present text—perhaps even the telescoping of a two-part play into a play of five acts.

For the authorship of *Cromwell* I can offer no suggestion which can be supported by any semblance of proof. We know, of course, that for the plays on Cardinal Wolsey, Philip Henslowe in 1601 made payments to Henry Chettle, Michael Drayton, Anthony Munday, and Wentworth Smith. In the manuscript play of *Sir Thomas More* those qualified to speak with authority have without dissent recognized the handwriting of Munday, Chettle, and Dekker. As no sample of his handwriting has survived for comparison, it is not impossible that one of the two unidentified hands in *More* is that of Wentworth Smith, but Chettle and Munday are the two who, we can confidently say, collaborated in both plays. Henslowe's payments seem to indicate that Chettle was the principal author in the Wolsey plays; Munday is recognized as the principal author of *Sir Thomas More*. A successful play on any one of three great chancellors of Henry VIII might well suggest to its authors, or to others, the advisability of a play dealing with another of the chancellors. The transfer to More of a jest originally attributed to Cromwell indicates that the authors were not unread in the career of a chancellor other than that with whom they were then dealing. The incident of the long-haired ruffian appears in *More* in the handwriting of Munday and is found again in his and Chettle's *Death of Robert, Earl of Huntingdon* (1598), IV, i; as has been noted, it had earlier been told of Cromwell in Foxe's *Acts and Monuments,* the principal source of *Thomas Lord Cromwell.* Indeed, there is much in the story of Cromwell which might have attracted the interest and sympathy of Anthony Munday. Munday and Cromwell shared the same passion for foreign travel, and Cromwell's being robbed and stripped by highwaymen in Italy was an experience almost identical to that which Munday in *The English Romayne Lyfe* and in *The Mirrour of Mutability* reports that he himself had suffered.[29] Again, Munday, with his militant Protestantism and his frequent anti-Catholic activities, might certainly have been attracted to the story of one credited with having pulled down the abbeys and changed the religion of the land. Had he dealt with the career of Cromwell, we should expect to find in his treatment the same idealization and sentimentality apparent in the present tragedy.

For Munday's participation in *Thomas Lord Cromwell,* then, it may be said that his collaboration in *More* and *Wolsey* indicates his interest in the rise and fall of the great figures under Henry VIII, that he had apparently read Foxe's life of Cromwell, on which the tragedy of *Cromwell* was based, and that there is every reason to believe that he would have been exceptionally interested in the career of one whose views he so obviously shared and some of whose experiences had duplicated his own. If Munday did participate in the writing of *Thomas Lord Cromwell*, it may well have been that he had for collaborators some of the same dramatists who had worked with him on *More* and/or *Wolsey*. Perhaps W. S.—Wentworth Smith—had a share. There is certainly little reason to think that Smith could have had the principal hand in an earlier and fuller account of the whole life and death of Thomas Lord Cromwell. If, however, he with Munday and others had collaborated in such an earlier play, perhaps a play in two parts, the explanation of the "W. S." on the title-page may be that as one of the original contributors Smith undertook, by telescoping or by cutting and pasting, to make suitable for the stage the earlier play or plays which the recent difficulties of the Earl of Essex had rendered highly unacceptable.

[3]

THE PURITAN
or, The Widow of Watling Street

OF THE THREE PLAYS which were on their title-pages ascribed to "W. S.," the last to be published and assuredly the last to be written was *The Puritan; or, the Widow of Watling Street*, entered to George Elde on 6 August 1607 and printed by him during the same year. Omitted from the folios of 1623 and 1632, *The Puritan* was first claimed as a work by Shakespeare in a list of plays offered for sale by the bookseller Archer in 1656; eight years later it was accepted into the canon of his work and published in the Third Folio. Since Malone's rejection of it, few critics except Tieck and Schlegel [1] have acepted the possibility of Shakespeare's participation in it in any way. The statement upon the title-page that it had been "Acted by the Children of Paules"—a statement supported by references within the play to the small size of the actors [2]—makes it almost certain that Shakespeare could have had no part in its composition. And that conclusion is supported both by the nature and quality of the play and by the date at which it must have been written. *The Puritan* is in many respects strikingly similar to several plays acted by the children's companies between 1604 and 1606; and a mere summary of its action is probably sufficient to convince most readers that Shakespeare could never have written it during the years he was writing *Lear, Macbeth,* and *Antony and Cleopatra.*

In scene i the widow, Lady Plus, mourns her husband who has just been buried. Refusing comfort, she firmly rejects the suggestion of her brother-in-law, Sir Godfrey, that she take a second husband. Her elder daughter, seeing her mother's grief, vows that she too will remain unmarried, but the younger, more lusty, declares that for one tear for a dead father she could give twenty kisses for a quick husband. The son, Edmond, says he is no such fool as to weep but will now enjoy his inheritance.

In the second scene George Pye-board, a scholar, and Skirmish, an old soldier, lament the hard times peace has brought to soldiers. That they may live by their wits, George suggests that he pose as a fortune-teller, Skirmish as a conjuror. The widow, he says, is an excellent subject to practice upon, her brother a gull, her son a fool, and her younger daughter an ape. Captain Idle is led across the stage on his way to prison, and George and Skirmish follow to learn how they may help him. Similarly one of the widow's servants, Nicholas, learns from Corporal Oath of the captain's imprisonment and, as he is the captain's kinsman, agrees to accompany the corporal to visit him (I, iii). In the following scene in the prison, Nicholas is persuaded to "nim" Sir Godfrey's chain and hide it in an arbor, and George instructs Skirmish and Oath that they that evening meet before the widow's house, pretend to quarrel, and draw their swords.

In II, i, the widow is visited by the knights who are suitors to her and her elder daughter, but dismisses them, declaring she will not remarry. George Pye-board enters.

He is, he says, no suitor, nor of those parts; he is a fortune-
teller, come to warn her that her late husband is in purga-
tory because of his evil practices and there must remain
unless she and her elder daughter change their minds about
not marrying and the younger daughter abandon her plan
of hasty marriage. To convince her of his powers, George
declares that her brother will soon suffer a loss and that
blood will be shed before her house that very day. In a
soliloquy he reports that he has instructed Skirmish to
wound the corporal in the leg, that he will then give the
latter a sleeping potion, and that after Skirmish is condemned for the murder of the sleeping corporal, he will
take it upon himself to raise the dead and so win further
credit.

After Nicholas has announced (II, ii) that he has secured
Sir Godfrey's chain and goes to hide it, the two soldiers
meet as agreed and in the presence of the widow's servants
quarrel and draw their swords. As the corporal is wounded,
George slips in and gives him a cordial containing a sleeping potion. Skirmish is arrested and the wounded corporal
carried off.

The widow is excited to learn (III, ii) that George's
prophecy is fulfilled. Sir Godfrey enters, raging at the loss
of his chain, and a servant announces that the corporal has
died. Questioned about the chain, Nicholas, as instructed
by George, declares that his cousin Captain Idle is a conjuror who, were he released from debtors' prison, could
certainly locate the chain. Sir Godfrey promises to have
Idle released.

The next two scenes (III, iii, iv), though they contribute
suspense, do not advance the plot but present rather an
interlude in which Pye-board, arrested at the suit of his

hostess, outwits the officers of the law by declaring that he was on his way to receive pay for a masque he had just completed for a gentleman who lived nearby. Expecting a handsome fee, the sergeants agree to go with him to deliver the masque. George selects an imposing house and knocks at the door. When the gentleman is summoned, George, pretending to read him a portion of the masque, explains to the gentleman his distress and his device. The gentleman, pleased with the jest, invites Pye-board in to receive his money. After the sergeants have waited for some time, the gentleman reappears, expresses surprise that they are sheriff's men, and explains that George had left by a back door.

Again at the prison (III, v), George explains to the captain how he must conjure. After Sir Godfrey has paid his debts, the captain, prompted by George, who has learned from an almanac that there will be a storm the next day at noon, promises to recover the chain at that time. After the captain has with fake conjuring revealed where the chain is hidden (IV, ii), a servant announces a strange sight approaching—one to burying, another to hanging. It is of course the corporal, who is thought dead, and Skirmish, who is to be hanged for murder. Knowing that the effect of the potion will soon have worn off, George orders the sheriff to set down the corpse (IV, iii), declaring that unless he can awaken the dead man, he will suffer for the condemned. The corporal comes to with an oath, and all are invited within to a feast. The elder daughter remains on stage to tell of her love for Pye-board.

The first scene of Act V presents the excited preparations for a double wedding, that of the widow to the conjuring captain and that of her elder daughter to George Pye-board.

Skirmish, however, feeling deserted by his former friends, has revealed George's various deceits to the earlier suitors, and one of them, Sir Oliver Muck-hill, has summoned to his aid a nobleman whom, to do his bidding, he keeps in his debt. In the concluding scene the nobleman stops the wedding procession, reveals the deceits practiced upon them, and advises the women to accept the knights as husbands. They do.

Although mildly amusing here and there, *The Puritan* is in no sense a distinguished play. Aside from its once having been regarded as a work by William Shakespeare, its chief claim to interest today would be as another illustration of the boldness of the early Jacobean playwrights and actors in presenting the controversial issues of their day. The play is larded with topical allusions; most of them are to be found in other plays of the period and, though they do perhaps enable us to date the play with greater confidence, they reveal little originality on the part of the playwright. There are references to John Stow the chronicler, Derecke the hangman, George Stone the bear; to the Brownists and the silencing of ministers of Puritan sympathies; to King James's promiscuous creation of knights and his unpopular effort to unite the two realms of England and Scotland under the name of Great Britain. Although the period in which we might expect to find any of these allusions seems to extend over a number of years, they doubtless assist in supporting other more definite evidence of the date at which *The Puritan* was written.

In III, v, 290–92, one of the characters says while turning the pages of the almanac, "*Iune–Iulie:* here, Iulie; thats this month. Sunday thirteene, yester day forteene,

to day fifteene." Fleay pointed out that July 15 fell on
Tuesday in 1606. The day of the week or of the month
could, of course, be easily changed to fit any particular
year in which the play might be revived, but one may well
question whether as a rule such corrections would be made
in the theatre copy.

A date of composition within 1605 or 1606 would seem
to be suggested by many topical allusions within the play.
Presumably no earlier than 1605 could Gentleman's speech
in III, iv, 184, have read "I protest he receivde all of me
in Brittaine gold of the last coyning." On the first coins
minted after James ascended the English throne he is styled
Iacobus D. G. Ang. Sco. Fran. et Hib. Rex. During the
second year of his reign, however, James assumed the title
of King of Great Britain, and an indenture was executed
11 November 1604 for a coinage whereon the king's new
title was to be adopted, *Mag. Brit.* to be substituted for
Ang. Sco.[3] The gold coins issued during King James's
reign bear no dates, but it would seem unlikely that the
new British coins were in circulation before 1605. Similarly any humor derived from the topical reference in "Brittaine gold of the last coyning" would seem to depend upon
the new British coins being recent enough still to excite
interest.

King James's efforts to unite the realms of England and
Scotland under the name of Britain may be again glanced
at in V, i, when Pye-board and Captain Idle, expecting to
be married that morning, enter dressed as bridegrooms.
The widow's son observes "Oh, how brauely they are shot
vp in one night; they looke like fine Brittaines now, me
thinkes." Perhaps "Brittaines" here is equivalent to Scots,
to the carpet-baggers similar to Andrew Lethe in Middle-

ton's *Michaelmas Term,* whose fortunes, once they had
reached England, seemed to many of the English to shoot
up in one night. But there is probably also a reference to
King James's desire to unite the two nations into one—a
reference similar to that to be seen in Edward Sharpham's
The Fleire (printed 1607 and usually dated 1606), where
a character is made to say, "I did pray often when I was an
Englishman, but I have not praid often, I must confesse,
since I was a Brittaine." [4]

Neither of these references to "Brittaine" appears in-
compatible with 1606 as the date of the composition of
The Puritan, although they might not be unexpected in
1605 or late 1604. The same may be said of the allusion to
"the Act past in Parliament against Coniurers and Witches"
(III, v, 160–61), enacted by James's first parliament in
1604, or of the satire upon King James's indiscriminate
creation of knights. To be sure James had been in England
scarcely four months before his promiscuous bestowal or
sale of knighthood was bitterly commented on, and this
bitter comment continued for several years, reaching its
bitterest stage perhaps in late 1605 and 1606. *The Puritan*
contains much satire of the fools and knaves who had been
granted knighthood. The widow, Lady Plus, laments the
knight her late husband as one who "would deceaue all
the world to get riches" and who had overthrown "the
right heyre of those lands" he had acquired. Sir Godfrey,
the widow's brother-in-law, urging that she take a second
husband, asks "what should wee doe with all our Knights,
I pray, but to marry riche widdowes?" (I, i, 86). The
names of the suitors to the widow and her daughters
suggest the degradation to which knighthood had fallen:
Sir Andrew Tipstaffe, Sir Oliver Muck-hill, and Sir John

Penny-dub, the latter of whom, Penny-dub, is described
as a knight of the last feather, "the son of a most abhomina-
ble father," and to suggest still further his purchase of his
title, is made to ask, "what, do you thinke I was dubd for
nothing? no, by my faith" (IV, i, 4–5).

Except for the reference to Tuesday, July 15, peculiar
to the year 1606, the allusions so far noted, though they
might well still have been timely in 1606, support for *The
Puritan* a date hardly more restricted than "after late
1604." Other allusions may, however, argue for a later
date.

Of questionable value, certainly, is the allusion to the
bear, George Stone. Referring to his arrest for debt, Pye-
board asks the Captain: . . . "how many Dogges doe you
thinke Ide vpon me?"

Capt. Dogs? I say? I know not.
Pyb. Almost as many as *George Stone* the Beare: Three at once,
     three at once. (III, v, 13–17)

Admittedly the reference to George Stone's being baited by
something more than three dogs at a time may refer to
more than one occasion, even indeed to the usual practice.
Yet it is possible that the reference is to George's last and
fatal appearance. As is learned from a petition to the king
by Philip Henslowe, then Keeper of the King's Bears,
at a baiting "before the kinge of denmarke," who was in
England during late July and early August of 1606, he
"loste a goodlye beare called gorge stone." [5]

Because the reference to Tuesday July 15 fits only 1606,
because King Christian of Denmark arrived in England to
visit his brother-in-law during the same week of July
1606, and because it may be assumed that at a baiting in

honor of a visiting king greater risks than usual were taken with the bears, it is not impossible that Pye-board is re-ferring to George Stone's being finally killed by over-whelming odds.

Hardly more certain is the identification of a passage in *The Puritan* as an allusion to *Macbeth*, which, if allowed, would seem to date the comedy no earlier than late 1606. Elated by what he regards as truly miraculous acts by Pye-board and the captain, the recovery of his lost chain and the apparent raising of the dead corporal, Sir Godfrey at the end of IV, iii, invites all present to a banquet:

I, and a banquet ready by this time, Maister Sheriffe, to which I most cheerefully enuite you, and your late prisoner there. See you this goodly chaine, sir? mun, no more words, twas lost, and is found againe; come, my inestimable bullies, weele talke of your noble Acts in sparkling Charnico, and in stead of a Iester, weele ha the ghost ith white sheete sit at vpper end a' th Table.

It is certainly not beyond question that there is an in-tended allusion to the ghost of Banquo in Sir Godfrey's promise to "ha the ghost ith white sheete sit at vpper end a' th Table." His remark springs naturally from the situa-tion. Others than Sir Godfrey refer to the corporal as a ghost, both because all but Pye-board, who had adminis-tered the sleeping potion, assume that he has been raised from the dead and because he had, preparatory to burial, been wrapped in a winding sheet, as is evident from his first remark upon waking: "Zounes; where am I? couered with Snow?" As the whole situation is part of the plan prepared by Pye-board and as no device is more common among Elizabethan dramatists than the clearing of the stage by an invitation to dinner, it seems by no means certain that we have here a deliberate reference to the appearance of Banquo's ghost at Macbeth's feast. On the other hand, the startling effectiveness of the banquet scene in *Macbeth*, more clearly alluded to in *The Knight of the Burning Pestle* (1607?), might tempt one to see an allusion here if it could be proved that *The Puritan* was the later play.

A date no earlier than 1606 could be definitely established for *The Puritan* if it could be shown that the dramatist drew upon *The Merry Conceited Jests of George Peele*, which was entered upon the Stationers' Register on 14 December 1605 [6] and presumably printed shortly thereafter, although the earliest extant edition of the *Jests* carries the date 1607. As the great majority of the jests which appear in this brief pamphlet had previously been related of others,[7] very few of them could have had any foundation in the actual escapades of George Peele, Master of Arts from Oxford, dramatist and "the very artifex of poetry," who had died about 1597. The compiler simply brought together a number of jests, mostly time-worn, although his doing so is probably to be explained by Peele's enjoying the reputation of a man of wit and many shifts. The scholar of *The Puritan*, George Pye-board, was, of course, intended to be recognized as George Peele. A "peele" is a "pie-board," and is defined by Webster as "a spadelike implement, variously used, as for removing loaves of bread, etc., from a baker's oven." It may seem not impossible that the jests of George Pye-board as presented in *The Puritan* provided the original suggestion for a jestbook and that the compiler, taking two jests from the play, hastily brought together a number of others, some perhaps based on stories told of Peele, others previously unconnected with him.

Neither is it impossible that the two jests common to the play and the jestbook had been often recounted orally and had reached dramatist and compiler each independently of the other. One of the two jests, at least, seems to appear in *The Puritan* in an earlier form than in the jestbook. Jest 2 of the latter, which closely parallels the trick by which Pye-board outsmarts the sergeants in III, iii and iv, relates how George, having borrowed and then absconded with the lute of a barber of Brentford, is followed by the barber to London. Explaining that a gentleman had borrowed the lute from him, Peele agrees to go with the barber to fetch it. They go to the house of an alderman, where Peele is welcomed by the porter, to whom he was well known as he "at that time had all the oversight of the pageants."

George goes directly to the alderman, who now is come into the court, in the eye of the barber; where George . . . draws a black [blank?] paper out of his bosom, and making action to the barber, reads the alderman as followeth. "I humbly desire your worship to stand my friend in a slight matter. Yonder hard-favoured knave . . . hath dogged me to arrest me. . . . The occasion is but trivial. . . . Therefore, this is my boon; that your worship would let one of your servants let me out at the garden gate [8]

The jest is much better told in the play, where the greedy sergeants render the audience more sympathetic to the scholar. There, as Pye-board claims to have with him a masque written at the command of the gentleman, it is understandable why he should produce a paper and pretend to read from it; it is less clear why he should do so when he has merely come to ask the return of a lute. A connection between the two accounts may, however, be suggested by Peele's identifying the barber as one that "hath dogged me to arrest me" and Pye-board's asking "how many Dogges doe you thinke Ide vpon me?"

The second trick appearing in both the play and the jest-book would appear clearly to be in an earlier form in the jestbook. There in Jest 11 Peele, as an Oxford M. A., is urged by three friends to accompany them to an Oxford commencement. When they have half completed the trip, George, lacking money, secretly hides the gilt rapier and dagger of one of his companions; then, borrowing forty shillings from his victim, he rides to Oxford to secure the aid of a scholar whom he declares to be "one of the rarest men in England." Upon their return, the scholar, assuming a distracted countenance and uttering strange words, declares that the rapier is "northeast, enclosed in wood near the earth." All search until George finds it where he had hidden it. This trick is, of course, much more elaborately presented in IV, ii, of the play, where the perpetrators are declared to be "two of the rarest men within the walls of Christendom!"

As the jestbook is merely a collection of brief accounts of jests said to have been practiced by Peele, for the most part unrelated, its compiler, if borrowing from the play, would have had no reason to alter the details of any jest or to change the place in which it was performed. The dramatist, on the contrary, would have had to introduce such changes as would make the jests accord with his other material. It would appear much more likely, therefore, that the playwright borrowed from the jestbook than that its compiler borrowed from the play. There must remain, however, the possibility that the two jests attributed to

Peele were common knowledge, that both compiler and dramatist heard independently through oral transmission the two escapades which they both present.

For assigning to *The Puritan* a date of composition no earlier than 1606 there are, then, four reasons: the probable but uncertain use by the dramatist of *The Merry Conceited Jests of George Peele*, licensed in December 1605; the reference to Tuesday, July 15th, suitable only to 1606; a possible but again uncertain allusion to the last baiting of George Stone, which took place in late July or early August of the same year; and finally a possible though hardly unquestionable allusion to the banquet scene in *Macbeth*. Urging the acceptance of at least some of these reasons, there appears to be evidence of a different and, I should think, most unexpected sort—a personal attack upon two churchmen which could not have been made prior to 1605.

One of the chief features of *The Puritan*, though lost in such a summary as I gave, is the bitterness in the attacks upon the Puritans. There are repeated references to their hypocrisy and to their fondness for long sermons. Lady Plus's first husband, affectionately described by her as one who had overthrown the rightful heir to get lands and who "would deceaue all the world to get riches" (I, i), would, she says, "keepe Church so duly; rise early, before his seruants, and e'en for Religious hast, go vngartered, vnbuttoned, nay, sir Reuerence, vntrust, to Morning Prayer. . . . Dine quickly vpon hie-dayes, and when I had great guests, would e'en shame me and rize from the Table, to get a good seate at an after-noone Sermon" (II, i, 231–39).

"Oh," adds the scholar, "a Sermon's a fine short cloake

of an houre long, and wil hide the vpper-part of a dissembler. Church! I, he seem'd al Church, & his conscience was as hard as the Pulpit."

Similarly ridiculed are the Puritans' fear of a well-rounded oath and their literal interpretation of the Commandments. The Puritan servants are terrified by the corporal's oaths, and one of them, Frailty, is made to say "We may lie, but we must not sweare" (I, iii, 75); and Nicholas almost swoons when it is suggested that he steal his master's chain ". . . had it beene to rob, I would ha don't; but I must not steale: that's the word, the literall, *thou shalt not steale*" (I, iv, 162–65). He readily agrees, of course, to "nim" the chain.

The full title of the play is *The Puritan; or, the Widow of Watling Street.* The neighborhood of Watling Street, from St. Paul's Cathedral to the Mansion House, was a section heavily inhabited by Puritans. Lady Plus, her children, her brother-in-law, and her servants are all said to be of the society or brotherhood of Puritans. The servants are named Nicholas St. Antlings, Frailty, and Simon St. Mary Overies. The name of the first servant was clearly drawn from the church which stood in Watling Street at the north side of Budge Row, St. Antlings (or St. Antholins), a center of Puritanism, later described by Dugdale as "the grand nursery whence most of the seditious preachers were after sent abroad throughout England to poyson the people with their antimonarchial principles." [9] Just as clearly the name of the third servant, Simon St. Mary Overies, was derived from the church on the south bank of the Thames, now Southwark Cathedral but in the sixteenth and seventeenth centuries generally known as St. Mary Overies. The corporal, who is, to be sure, "a Vaineglorious fellow," addresses the servants as "Puritanicall Scrape-shoes, Flesh a good Fridayes . . . you halfe-Christened *Katomites,* you vngod-mothered Varlets" (I, iii, 11–17). The minister at St. Antlings is twice referred to as Mr. Pigman (I, i, 22; V, i, 12), and it is presumably to him that Nicholas refers when he sends word to his master that he has gone "to a Fast . . . with Maister *Fulbellie* the Minister":

Sim[*on*]. Maister *Ful-bellie?* an honest man: he feedes the flock well, for he's an excellent feeder.
Fray[*lty*]. O, I, I haue seene him eate vp a whole Pigge, and afterward falle to the pettitoes. (I, iii, 84–90)

Nicholas makes a further reference to his minister—presumably the minister of St. Antlings: "our Parson," he says, "railes againe Plaiers mightily, I can tell you, because they brought him drunck vpp'oth Stage once,—as hee will bee horribly druncke" (I, iv, 208–11). No play of the period survives in which a Puritan minister is brought drunk upon the stage, nor need one assume, as did Professor Creizenach, "that a drunken Puritan minister appeared in a play now lost." [10] Nor, certainly, should we be justified in assuming that the author of *The Puritan* is here truly picturing the gross habits of one particular minister, the then incumbent in the Church of St. Antlings. I suspect, however, that there can be little doubt that he is in the names he assigns the servants making a direct thrust at two identifiable ministers who had perhaps aroused his ire.

Two of the three Puritan servants are called, as has been said, Nicholas St. Antlings and Simon St. Mary Overies. It can hardly be mere coincidence that the minis-

ter at St. Antlings from 1592 to 1617 was Nicholas Felton
and that at St. Mary Overies, where "until recent years"
"the church was served by two 'Preaching Chaplains' "
instead of a rector, one of the two chaplains appointed in
1605 was William Symonds.[11] Of both Felton and Symonds there are accounts in the *Dictionary of National
Biography*, but these accounts offer no suggestion why the
dramatist should have chosen to name the stupid, hypo-
critical Puritan servants after the ministers of the two
churches, Nicholas (Felton) St. Antlings and (William)
Symon(ds) St. Mary Overies. Neither divine is known to
have been active in the attacks upon the stage, nor, so far
as is known, were they militant Puritans.

Symonds, who was a chaplain at St. Mary Overies for
several years and who is described in Wood's *Athenae
Oxonienses* as "a person of an holy life, grave and moderate in his carriage, painful in the ministry, well learned,
and of rare understanding in prophetical scriptures," [12]
was the author of three publications listed in the *Short
Title Catalogue: Pisgah Evangelica:* a commentary upon
the book of Revelation, 1605; *A Heavenly Voice:* a sermon, 1606; and *Virginia:* a sermon preached at White-
chapel in the presence of the adventurers and planters for
Virginia, 25 April 1609. He helped Captain John Smith
in the publication of his *General History of Virginia* and is
thought to have been for a while resident in that colony.
His printed works reveal no attack upon the stage; they
suggest rather ecclesiastical conformity, his bitterness being directed principally against the Papists and occasionally
against the Brownists. His two earlier works are addressed
to Richard Vaughan, bishop of London, whose "tenure of
the bishopric was marked by the deprivation and silencing

of extreme puritans," [13] although John Chamberlain noted that in that "course he hath won himself great commendation of gravity, wisdom, learning, mildness and temperance, even amongst that faction." [14] In the letter to Bishop Vaughan prefacing *A Heavenly Voice*, dated 25 January 1606, Symonds suggests that he had before then been subjected to calumny: he asks that his lordship extend him his "fatherly and Christian patronage" and "defend me frō the cauils and calumnations of the contentious, (of whose fury I haue had too much experience:) . . ." [15] Presumably, however, the reference here is not to the attack upon him in *The Puritan* unless that play is to be dated in 1605—a date too early to allow the use of *The Merry Conceited Jests*, the allusion to *Macbeth*, the aptness of the mention of Tuesday, July 15. But even if Symonds' reference be not to *The Puritan*, it clearly declares that he had prior to the opening of 1606 suffered calumnies of some fury. That he previously had been the subject of "cauils and calumnations" may well support if not explain the dramatist's choosing to name his quibbling hypocrite Symon(ds) St. Mary Overies.

Nicholas Felton, who was born in the same year as Symonds, 1556, had a more distinguished career, becoming bishop of Bristol, Master of Pembroke, and later bishop of Bath and Wells. According to the *Dictionary of National Biography*:

Felton's exact theological position is not easy to determine. He left no writings, and little is recorded by his contemporaries of any part taken by him in the controversies of the day. Puritan sympathies have been attributed to him, because . . . [some] of his curates and chaplains were of [that] theological school. An opposite inference may be drawn from his close and confidential friendship with [Bishop] Andrews.

Felton seems indeed to have been a moderate. Bishop Andrews, urging his election to the Mastership of Pembroke, declared his "most worthy, upright and learned friend" one likely to "heal the dissensions then long prevailing, and prove a good head to a good house else likely to sink"; [16] and Fuller records that he had "a sound head and a sanctified heart, was beloved of all good men, very hospitable to all, and charitable to the poor." [17]

Although it could hardly have been accident or other than deliberate design that led the dramatist to the selection of the first names of Nicholas St. Antlings and Simon St. Mary Overies, I suspect one would be unjustified in seeking any further portrayal of the two ministers within the two servants. The servants, indeed, although of like hypocrisy, differentiate between their minister and themselves when they speak of him as one who "railes againe Plaiers mightily." Perhaps both Felton and Symonds had in their sermons expressed views which the dramatist regarded as attacks upon the players, or perhaps they had earned the dislike of the dramatist only by supporting or failing to take exception to attacks by others delivered from the pulpits of St. Antlings and St. Mary Overies. But surely in London of 1606 the attack upon the two clergymen could not have passed unrecognized.

Though no clear record survives of contemporary recognition of the attack upon the ministers, the actors did not escape censure for their ridicule of the two churches. It was clearly to *The Puritan* that the Reverend William Crashaw referred when, more than a year after the play must have been acted, he attacked the impudence of the

players in a *Sermon preached at the Cross,* 14 February
1607/8. The actors, he declared,

grow worse and worse, for now they bring religion and holy
things vpon the stage: no maruel though the worthiest and
mightiest men escape not, when God himselfe is so abused. Two
hypocrites must be brought foorth: and how shall they be described but by these names, *Nicholas S. Antlings, Simon S.
Maryoveries.* Thus hypocrisie a child of hell must beare the names
of two Churches of God, and two wherein Gods name is called
on publikely euery day in the yeere, and in one of them his blessed
word preached eucrie day . . . : yet these two, wherin Gods
name is thus glorified, and our Church and State honoured, shall
bee by these miscreants thus dishonoured, and that not on the
stage only, but even in print.[18]

When Crashaw declared it "no maruel though the worthiest . . . men escape not," he may have had the attack
upon the two ministers in mind; in a later sermon he de-
plores that the actors in their impudence "play with Princes
and Potentates, Magistrates and Ministers, nay with God
and Religion, and all holy things." [19]

Although there is little evidence either pro or con, one
may wonder whether the actors may not, by acting *The
Puritan,* have brought upon themselves a more severe
reprimand than the belated blast by William Crashaw. The
title-page, it will be recalled, states that the play had been
"Acted by the Children of Paules." "The last traceable
appearance of the Paul's boys was on 30 July 1606," when
they presented a lost play, *The Abuses,* before King James
and his brother-in-law, King Christian of Denmark. *The
Account of Denmark's Welcome,* printed in 1606, states
that "the Kinges seemed to take delight [in] and be much
pleased" by this performance. As no later record of the

company has been found and as no fewer than ten of their plays reached the printers in 1607 and 1608, Sir Edmund Chambers thought that the Children of Paul's must have discontinued acting soon after the July performance before their majesties.[20] No reason for the discontinuance of the company has ever been offered. One may ask, therefore, whether their performance of *The Puritan* shortly after July 1606 may not have contributed to their suppression. Obviously it would ill become a company of actors, even though related to St. Paul's Cathedral in little more than name, to ridicule two neighboring time-honored churches such as St. Antlings and St. Mary Overies, and surely the Puritans would not have been alone in condemning such an act.

On the other hand, Crashaw's sermon at the Cross seems rather to suggest that the players had not been punished for their impudence, for if they had been punished, if the company had been suppressed for acting *The Puritan,* his tirade would have had little point and less justification. The date of his sermon and his reference to the play's being in print may indicate that Crashaw got his knowledge of the play by reading it, but it would seem unlikely that he should not have learned of it—at least before he printed the sermon—had the company been disciplined because of their performance.

Although W. S. are the initials of one of those I think held up to ridicule in *The Puritan,* William Symonds, chaplain of St. Mary Overies, I shall not suggest that the "By W. S." of the title-page was the result of a misreading or misunderstanding of an earlier "at W. S." A similar suggestion was offered by Fleay and enthusiastically appropriated by Hopkinson, who declared that

One of the main purposes of the play was to imitate, parody, or burlesque Shakespeare's works; that object is so clear and so prominent that it is impossible to evade the conclusion. The allusions to, and imitations of, Shakespeare's plays are too numerous to be given here; a few are to be found in the notes of my reprint of the play, 1894, and more in Malone's "Supplement," 1780, and Mr. Fleay's 'Biographical Chronicle of the English Drama.' [21]

Steevens, fresh from editing the plays of Shakespeare, did contribute to the edition of *The Puritan* published in the *Supplement* a large number of verbal parallels between it and the plays of Shakespeare, including some Shakespearean plays which postdate *The Puritan;* but, though he thought the author of the latter must have been familiar with Shakespeare's work, he expressed no suspicion that Shakespeare was parodied or burlesqued. Fleay produced few if any additional parallels; Hopkinson, as far as I could tell, none.

When in IV, iii of *The Puritan,* some thirty lines after the coffin bearing the sleeping corporal is brought in, Pyeboard says to the Sheriff, "Let me entreate the corps to be set downe," and the Sheriff replies, "Bearers, set downe the Coffin," few, surely, can take seriously Fleay's confident statement that the situation and language here were but a travesty of *Richard III*, I, ii, where Richard interrupts the funeral procession of King Henry VI:

> *Rich.*   Stay, you that bear the corse, and set it down.
> *Anne.*   What black magician conjures up this fiend
> To stop devoted charitable deeds?
> *Rich.*   Villains, set down the corse; or by St. Paul,
> I'll make a corse of him that disobeys.

Although in both plays a funeral procession is interrupted, the situations in the two plays are radically different; and the verbal similarity extends no further than the appearance in both passages of the words "set down" and "corpse." And certainly it is equally absurd to see in Pye-board's "How now! for shame, for shame, put vp, put vp," as he pretends to seek to stop the fight between Oath and Skirmish (III, i), a parody or burlesque of the Hostess' speech in 2 *Henry IV*, after Falstaff has driven Pistol downstairs: "Alas, alas; put up your naked weapons, put up your naked weapons" (II, iv).

How worthless are most of the "Shakespearean echoes" which have been suggested is indicated by the various editors of *The Shakespeare Allusion Book* having excluded all save that to Banquo's ghost, previously discussed. One other, however, deserves consideration. Steevens noted that in III, i, of *The Puritan* there

is an odd agreement with a few circumstances . . . in the last act of *Othello* . . . Pyeboard (Iago) advises Skirmish (Roderigo) to wound Oath (Cassio). In the confusion occasioned by this attempt, Pyeboard (Iago again) rushes among them, and instead of giving Oath (Cassio again) assistance, prepares somewhat to make him seem dead. Thus Iago wounds Cassio. The cut too is given on the *leg;* and Pyeboard takes on him the cure, as Iago comes out and proffers to bind up Cassio's wound.

What happened in *The Puritan* seems clear enough, for in an earlier soliloquy Pye-board had informed us:

I haue aduizde old *Peter Skirmish,* the souldier, to hurt Corporall *Oth* vpon the Leg; and in that hurry Ile rush amongst 'em, and in stead of giuing the Corporal some Cordiall to comfort him, Ile power into his mouth a potion of a sleepy Nature, to make him seems as dead; for the which the old souldier beeing apprehended, and ready to bee borne to execution, Ile step in, & take vpon me the cure of the dead man . . . (II, i, 339–48)

In *The Puritan,* then, it is Skirmish (Roderigo) who wounds Oath (Cassio). What happens in *Othello,* however, is far from clear. Although neither the quarto nor the Folio text of *Othello* indicates that Iago rushes from his hiding place to wound Cassio, all editors have accepted Theobald's stage direction requiring him to do so; and doubtless all will agree that he should have done so whether or not Shakespeare so intended. Presumably Iago is on stage with Roderigo, hides himself at Cassio's entry, rushes forward to wound Cassio, and immediately makes his exit to return only after others have entered, aroused by the cries of the wounded men. In *The Puritan,* having reported in soliloquy his instructions to old Skirmish, Pye-board enters only as the corporal is wounded, and hastily proffers the potion. Perhaps we may think of him as lurking, like Iago, in the background and coming forward at the point at which the stage direction indicates entry, although the action here takes place shortly after five o'clock on a July afternoon, not as in *Othello* "between twelve and one" at night. Clearly it is not Pye-board who wounds the corporal in the leg; but neither is there in the early texts of *Othello* any suggestion that it was Iago and not Roderigo who wounds Cassio. Immediately after the corporal is wounded, Pye-board steals off stage as officers enter, and, unlike Iago, returns only after the two combatants have been carried off.

There is certainly a considerable similarity in the two scenes, and it appears not impossible that the situation in *The Puritan* was indeed in part suggested by that in

Othello; yet there seems insufficient reason to regard it as a parody or even as intended to call to mind the more diabolical stratagem of Iago. If, however, the author of *The Puritan* be recognized as indebted to *Othello,* there may be greater reason to believe that he was thinking of *Macbeth* when he had Sir Godfrey promise to "ha the ghost ith white sheete sit at vpper end a' th Table."

The play's alliterative sub-title, *The Widow of Watling Street,* may derive from a broadside ballad both parts of which were entered on the Stationers' Register 15 August 1597.[22] To this broadside, however, the play owes little else. Part I of the ballad narrates how a father, tired of his son's evil practices, had refused to release him from debtors' prison but is persuaded by his wife to name him co-executor with her of his will. Upon the death of the father the son, by accusing his mother for a harlot and his sisters for bastards, seeks to secure the whole estate for himself. In Part II the widow appeals to the Council, whose sober countenances so frighten the false witnesses the son has gathered that they confess their earlier perjury. The son, sent to prison, hangs himself.

Slight indeed is the similarity to the play. In both a recently made widow, a parishioner of St. Antlings, has daughters and one son who has no affection for his father. The one likeness worthy of comment is perhaps that both sons claim to know the law. The son in the ballad, recognizing that a widow is allowed one-third of her husband's moveables, at first declares:

> I graunt what lawe doth craue;
> But not a penny more will I
> discharge of any legasye (stanza 16);

and Edmond, in a soliloquy closing the first scene of the play, declares:

I know the law in that point; no Atturney can gull me. . . . Ile rule the Roast my selfe . . . the Lawe's in mine owne hands now: nay, now I know my strength, Ile be strong inough for my Mother, I warrant you.

The implication of Edmond's speech is certainly that he will at once proceed to try to secure for himself the greater part of his father's estate. But he does not do so, and as the play progresses he bears no further resemblance to the son in the ballad. That he should, however, speak such lines in so emphatic a place as a soliloquy which closes the opening scene, suggests that the dramatist may at first have intended to give Edmond a more prominent role in the play and one more nearly resembling that of the wicked son of the ballad.

Richard Simpson has been, I believe, the only critic of the past hundred years or more to accept Shakespeare's authorship of *The Puritan*. In a paper prepared for the New Shakespeare Society,[23] Simpson urged a view never I suppose entertained by another, that in the three plays *The Puritan, The London Prodigal,* and *A Yorkshire Tragedy* Shakespeare was in turn attacking three of his early detractors, the university wits George Peele, Robert Greene, and Thomas Nash. Even if Shakespeare were known to have attacked Peele, the attack could hardly have been in *The Puritan* as that play is definitely stated to have been acted by a company for which Shakespeare is known never to have written.

Malone and Hazlitt nominated Wentworth Smith and W. Smith as author of *The Puritan,* but so little is known about those elusive playwrights that modern critics have not unnaturally sought the author among the dramatists known to have been writing for the Children of Paul's in the years around 1606.

As many of the *Jests* and other references to Peele indicate that his connections with and love for Oxford were widely known, it is conceivable that one dramatizing fictitious incidents in his career might, in an effort to secure a greater semblance of truth, deliberately seek out and introduce bits of Oxford slang into his dialogue; but since Farmer first pointed out the appearance of such peculiarly Oxford terms in the play, it has been widely assumed that the author of *The Puritan* must have been at one time a student at Oxford. In the plays of two former members of that university, both known to have been writing for the Paul's boys around 1606, many similarities to *The Puritan* have been noted. The weight of critical opinion has inclined toward the authorship of Thomas Middleton; but largely because Middleton was not then known to have attended Oxford, Tucker Brooke in 1908 advanced a claim for John Marston, seeing an "extremely close affinity" between *The Puritan* and *Eastward Hoe*.[24] Most if not all of the characteristics he cites as common to the two plays are, however, to be found in equal clarity in the plays of Thomas Middleton; and now that Middleton's connection with Oxford has been established,[25] his must, I believe, be regarded as the principal claim. His authorship of *The Puritan* has been urged by Fleay, Bullen, Hopkinson, and Ward, among others, and most recently by Professor W. D. Dunkel.[26]

Like the author of *The Puritan*—and, to be sure, other playwrights of his day—Middleton was especially inter-

ested in the contemporary scene. The most numerous and
by far the best of his plays are comedies of London life,
delightful comedies of fresh and ingenious intrigue and at
the same time sharp satires of what Middleton considered
the abuses, follies, and vices of Jacobean London: the Puritans, with an exterior of holiness and humility but within
greedy and lascivious; the carpet-baggers who had followed
the new king from Scotland, their vicious natures made
more vicious by their sudden fortunes; the cheating gallants who preyed upon the innocent; the merchants who
tricked young heirs into signing away their lands; the
lawyers, consuming the estates of their clients; the new-
made knights who had purchased knighthood before they
had attained the position of gentlemen.

To say that many of Middleton's London comedies are
constructed upon a formula would be an unfair exaggera-
tion, but it would not be altogether untrue. The comedies
are all comedies of intrigue, wherein the principal characters attain their ends by most ingeniously outwitting those
against whom they scheme, usurer, rival, parent or guardian. Not always, however, is the witty principal victorious
at the end; sometimes, though not often, like George Pye-
board he falls a victim to his own eager scheming. Though
Witgood in *A Trick to Catch the Old One* recovers the
lands he has pawned and the favor of his uncle by tricking
his uncle's enemy into marriage with a courtesan, in *A
Mad World, My Masters* Witgood's prototype, Follywit,
tricks himself into marriage with his grandfather's young
mistress. Yet it is always by tricks, by mad but purposeful
tricks, that Middleton's plots are advanced. It is in this respect that *The Puritan* is most reminiscent of Middleton's
comedies of London life. And it is this, plus its realistic

picture of London life and its pungent satire of similar
types, which has led many to urge Middleton's authorship
of *The Puritan*.

To strengthen their claim for Middleton's authorship
his advocates have called attention to a number of passages
which they think echo or parallel passages in Middleton's
accepted work. These are naturally of varying closeness,
and some of them, especially those revealing similarities
in technique, may be indicative; but by no means all argue
for identical authorship. By 1606 Middleton was a successful dramatist with a half dozen or so plays in the
repertory of the children's company. When in an anonymous play parallels are noted to the plays of Shakespeare,
borrowing is naturally and readily assumed; when, however, the similarities are to the plays of others, one has
been apt, perhaps too apt, to interpret them as the result
of an author's repeating himself.

As indicative of Middleton's authorship of *The Puritan* there has been cited a speech by Quomodo in *Michaelmas Term* (V, i, 63–65); "I knew a widow about Saint
Antlings so forgetful of her first husband, that she married again within the twelvemonth; nay, some, byrlady,
within the month." The "two points of resemblance" are
the parish of St. Antlings and the early remarriage of a
widow. But the speech could be cited as evidence against
as well as for Middleton's authorship of *The Puritan*. If
Quomodo is indeed referring to Lady Plus, he is strangely
understating the speed of her second marriage. The time
which elapses during the play is carefully indicated; Lady
Plus is betrothed to a second husband only five days after
the burial of her first. As Quomodo wishes by his remark
to suggest how quickly husbands are sometimes forgotten,

were the allusion to a play which Middleton had himself
written a short time before, one would expect Quomodo
to say, not "married again within a twelvemonth," but
"within a week." Neither is Lady Plus an illustration of the
inconstancy Quomodo had in mind. In her nor in her elder
daughter is there any suggestion of insincerity or inconstancy,
nor of the hypocrisy and the lasciviousness which Middleton
usually ascribes to Puritan women. Though they break their
oaths of a single life, they do so not because of weak or
lascivious natures. Their oaths are sincerely made and
strictly observed until the women are gulled by Pye-board's
carefully planned and executed tricks, and they accept husbands at the end only through the intervention of a *deus
ex machina* in the guise of an unnamed lord.

The two plays must have been written at about the same
time.[27] If *Michaelmas Term* were the later, the allusion to
Lady Plus, if such it be, rather than suggesting Middleton's
authorship of *The Puritan*, would argue that that play was
by another and that Middleton, when he introduced a
reference to it, recalled its argument but vaguely. If, on
the other hand, *The Puritan* were the later play, I can see
no reason to think Quomodo alluding to Lady Plus.

But I am neither prepared nor inclined to argue against
Middleton's authorship of *The Puritan*. The un-Middle-
tonian generosity to the Puritan women is doubtless demanded by the plot to underscore the cleverness required
in Pye-board's persuading them to ignore their vows. The
plot most certainly is one which would have appealed to
Middleton. I know no author to whose plays *The Puritan*
shows greater likeness.

A YORKSHIRE TRAGEDY

A Yorkshire Tragedy, having been entered to him upon the Stationers' Register on 2 May 1608, was printed for Thomas Pavier later in the same year and is both in the Stationers' Register entry [1] and on the title-page of the quarto declared to have been written by "W. Shakspeare." On the first page of the quarto the play is further identified as "All's one, or, one of the foure plaies in one, called A York-shire Tragedy as it was plaid by the Kings Maiesties Plaiers," while the title-page adds that it had been "Acted . . . at the Globe," and that it was in 1608 "Not so New as Lamentable and True."

It could not have been written more than three years before, because the murders which the play so vividly and accurately depicts had been perpetrated only in April 1605, near the town of Wakefield in Yorkshire. Walter Calverley, a gentleman of ancient and honorable family, had then, in a fit of madness, wounded his wife and slain two of his three children. It is noteworthy that (except for the servants appearing in scene i—clearly, I think, a later appendage) none of the characters in the play is identified by other than a type designation, Husband, Wife, Knight, Servant, and the like. All names of places, like those of the persons involved, are studiously omitted. Nothing except the title would lead us to associate the play with the Calverleys or indeed with Yorkshire were it not that the prominence of the Calverley family and the unnaturalness of the murders aroused sufficient excitement to provoke several other accounts which cite both names and places. Before the story was told in the 1607 edition of Stow's *Chronicles,* entries had been made upon the Stationers' Register, first, on 12 June 1605 of "A booke called Twoo Vnnaturall Murthers, the one practised by master *Coverley* a Yorkshire gent vppon his wife and happened on his children the 23 of Aprilis 1605" . . . ,[2] and on the third of the following month of "A ballad of Lamentable Murther Donne in Yorkshire by a gent vppon 2 of his owne Children sore woundinge his Wife and Nurse." [3] And after Calverley's execution, 5 August 1605, there was entered on the 24th of that month "The Arraignement Condempnacon and Execucon of Master Caverly at Yorke in August 1605." [4] No copy of the ballad or of the account of the execution is now known to exist, but fortunately the prose tract, *Two Unnatural Murthers,* has survived.

Entered on the Stationers' Register just seven weeks after the murders had occurred, it was beyond question the only source used by the dramatist. In reprinting this tract in 1863, John Payne Collier observed that "the drama and our tract correspond remarkably; but we do not trace any such particular coincidences of expression, as to lead us to suppose that the narrative was founded upon the play." [5] There can be no doubt that it was the play which was based upon the tract. Although the date at which the play was composed cannot be so definitely determined, the records reveal that only seven weeks elapsed between the murders and the entry of the tract for publication. The similarities of the two, in the general progress of the narrative and in specific wording, are so striking as to leave no doubt that one was prepared directly from a copy of the other. As the play was not printed until three years after the tract had appeared, it is unlikely that the author of the latter would have had access to the play—unless, of course, the same author was responsible for both. Even though there is that possibility, it would seem more likely that the author should construct the tragedy only after preparing a hurried prose account which could capitalize on the excitement and curiosity aroused by the murders. Again, although many of the details of the murders must certainly have been generally known, the author of the tract could not have got from the play the names of those figuring in the event, certain details of Calverley's earlier career, nor such insignificant and irrelevant details as that "at this time the infection of the plague was violente in Yorke" (Collier, p. 24); that the gaol to which Calverley was taken was "but lately built up in Wakefield" (p. 24); that when Calverley, having stabbed his eldest child, sought out the second, "the maide was dressing [the] childe by the fire" and, seeing the danger, "started from the fire" (p. 19); and, finally, that it was Calverley's "second brother" who was at the university and that the bond for which he had been imprisoned amounted to "a thousand pound" (p. 16). It would seem more likely that such minor and irrelevant details should have been omitted in a dramatization than that they should have been added in a narrative redaction.

Moreover, were the tract prepared from the play, the author of the former, relating the story in prose, would have had no need to make frequent transpositions or to substitute occasional synonyms in speeches which are almost identical to some in the play. On the other hand, the dramatist, especially when writing verse, would frequently have found it necessary to make such transpositions and substitutions as are to be seen in the excerpts which I shall quote.

Except for scene i, for which the tract offers merely a suggestion, every scene of the tragedy seems to have been based directly and solely upon the account in *Two Unnatural Murthers*. Again excepting scene i, everything presented in the play is found in the tract, and, save for such irrelevant details as noted, everything in the tract is to be found in the play. The tract runs to twenty-three and one-half pages in Collier's reprint. The first four pages the play wholly ignored, but the events and speeches recounted in the remaining pages were followed with little deviation. The extent to which the dramatist relies upon the tract and appropriates its wording may be seen from the excerpts that follow.

[*Wife*] . . . as you desire the three louely boyes you haue beene father vnto should grow vp . . . , acquaint me with your griefs . . . Maister *Cauerley* . . . delivered this: I now want money and thou must help me.

O! Master *Cauerley* (quoth she), though God and your selfe know I am no cause of your want, yet what I haue to supply you, either in iewels or rings, I pray you take; and I beseech you, as you are a gentleman, and by the loue you should beare to your children, although you care not for me, looke back a little into your estate . . . (*T.U.M.*, p. 8)

Wi. Show me the true cause of your discontent.
Hus. Mony, mony, mony, and thou must supply me.

Wi. Alas, I am the lest cause of your discontent,
  Yet what is mine, either in rings or Iewels,
  Vse to your own desire, but I beseech you,
  As y'are a gentleman by many bloods,
  Though I my selfe be out of your respect,
  Thinke on the state of these three louely boies
  You haue bin father to. (*A.Y.T.*, ii, 60–69)

[Wife] . . . my friends are fully possest your land is morgaged
. . . If you think I haue published any thing to him with desire to keepe the sale of my dowrie from you, either for mine
owne good or my childrens, though it fits I should haue a
motherly care of them (you being my husband), passe it away
how you please, spend it how you will, so I may enioy but welcome lookes, and kinde words from you. (*T.U.M.*, p. 15)

Wi. . . . . onely my friends
  Knew of our morgagde Landes, and were possesst
  Of euery accident before I came,
  If thou suspect it but a plot in me
  To keepe my dowrie, or for mine owne good
  Or my poore childrens: (though it sutes a mother
  To show a naturall care in their reliefs)
  Yet ile forget my selfe to calme your blood:
  Consume it, as your pleasure counsels you,
  And all I wishe eene Clemency affoords:
  Giue me but comely looks and modest wordes.
                          (*A.Y.T.*, iii, 65–75)

Now, sir, quoth Maister *Cauerley*, if you please but to walke
downe and see the grounds about my house, one of my men
shal goe along with you; at your returne I wil giue so sufficient
answer, that my brother by you shal be satisfied . . .

$$(T.U.M., p. 17)$$

Hus. Now, Sir, if you so please
    To spend but a fewe minuts in a walke
    About my grounds below, my man heere shall
    Attend you.
    I doubt not but by that time to be furnisht
    Of a sufficient answere, and therein
    My brother fully satisfied. (*A.Y.T.*, iv, 55–61)

This exact and direct borrowing from the tract is observable step by step and fact by fact in all the scenes of
the tragedy except the first, for which at most the tract
offers only a suggestion—a suggestion which is developed
in a way quite different from that in which material from
the tract is used in the nine later scenes. That portion of
the tract not used by the dramatist relates how Master
Calverley had, upon the death of his father, been placed
under the guardianship of a noble and worthy gentleman.
Because he possessed a substantial income and because "his
course of life did promise so much good, that there was a
commendable grauity appeared euen in his youth," young
Calverley was sought out by many gallant gentlemen and
especially by fathers who wished him to marry their daughters. At length a daughter of "an antient gentleman of
cheefe note in his country"

was by priuate assurance made Maister *Cauerleys* best beloued
wife: . . . yet in regard Maister *Cauerleys* yeeres could not
discharge his honourable gardian had ouer him, the father thought
it meete . . . to lengthen their desired haste, till . . . a fit
howre . . . Maister *Cauerley* hauing spent some time there in
decent recreation . . . with his new Mistresse, at last he be-
thought himselfe that his long stay made him long looked for at
London. . . . Maister *Cauerley* came to London, and whether
concealing his late contract from his honorable gardian, or for-
getting his priuate and publicke vowes, or both, I know not, but
Time . . . had not fanned ouer many daies, but hee . . . was
husband by all matrimoniall rites to a curteous gentlewoman, and
neere by marriage to that honourable personage to whom he was
ward.

Rumor . . . was not long in trauel before hee had deliuered
this distasted message to his first Mistresse eares, . . . This
gentlewoman . . . tooke . . . so to heart this vniust wrong,
that . . . shee brought her selfe to a consumption; . . . yet
vnder this yoake of griefe shee so paciently indured that . . .
shee only married these letters togither: I intreate of God to
grant both prosperous health and fruitfull wealth to him and his,
though I am sicke for his sake. (pp. 4–6)

The tract thereupon notes that "reuenge being alwaies in
Gods hand, thus it fel:" he "had not liued many months
with his wife, but . . . his actions did now altogether
practise the vnprofitable taste of vice . . . and in short
time so weakened his estate that . . . he grew into a discontent . . ." (pp. 6–7).

That this introductory material is easily adaptable to
the stage is seen by the use made of it in George Wilkins'
Miseries of Enforced Marriage, which will be discussed

later. To be sure, unless he had chosen to make use of a
dumb show or of a prologue, the dramatist could hardly
have presented all of this introductory material in as brief
a space as the ninety lines which make up scene i of *A
Yorkshire Tragedy*. What we find in this scene, however,
are merely unsatisfactory and thoroughly confusing scraps
of exposition, every one of which is totally unnecessary to
an understanding of what follows.

The opening stage direction of scene i reads *"Enter*
Oliuer *and* Ralph, *two seruingmen,"* the former observing that "my young Mistrisse is in such a pittifull passionate humor for the long absence of her loue." After
Ralph has conventionally compared maids to apples on a
tree, Oliuer asks "is neither our young maister returned,
nor our fellow Sam come from London?" Ralph has
scarcely answered "Neither" before he cries "Slidd, I
heare *Sam: Sam's* come," and Sam speaks off-stage of the
speed with which he has ridden, and entering, shows some
of the "tricks" he has brought from London. Again the
servingmen ask Sam what the news from London, and
Ralph adds, "My young mistresse keeps such a puling for
her loue."

Sam. Why, the more foole shee; I, the more ninny hammer shee.
Oli. Why, *Sam,* why?
Sam. Why, hees married to another Long agoe.
Ambo. Ifaith, ye Iest.
Sam. Why, did you not know that till now? why, hees married,
  beates his wife, and has two or three children by her . . .
Oli. Sirrah, Sam, I would not for two years wages, my yong
  mistres knew so much; sheed run vpon the left hand of her
  wit, and nere be her owne woman agen. (i, 45–61)

Sam reports further that the young master "has consumed al, pawnd his lands, and made his vniversitie brother stand in waxe for him . . . calls his wife whore . . . and his children bastards." But here, at line 72, Sam reverts to the souvenirs he has brought from London, and twenty-five lines later the three servants retire to sample the beer without mentioning other matters.

The dreadful inaptness of this opening scene is at once apparent to one reading the scenes that follow. First, there is the awkwardness about time; it would appear that the young mistress and the servants daily expect the return of the young master, although enough time has elapsed since his departure for him to have been married "long ago" and to have had "two or three children"—three as it turns out. Next there is confusion concerning the location in which scene i takes place. His marriage, his children, and his abusive treatment of his wife are reported presumably in Yorkshire as "newes from London" (lines 41ff.), and accordingly Mr. Tucker Brooke in his reprint of the play, following Malone and earlier editors, assigns this scene to "Calverley Hall"; yet it is quite apparent from the later scenes, as well as from the *Two Unnatural Murthers*, that Husband with his wife and children are not in London but are themselves living at Calverley Hall in Yorkshire. Again, as has been noted, in this scene alone are characters and dialogue introduced which had not been specifically mentioned in the tract followed so closely in all of the remaining scenes: not only are the characters who appear in this scene the only ones in the play to whom names are assigned, but they never again appear, nor are they or the young mistress of whom they speak ever again so much as referred to. We never learn whether she ran "vpon the lefte hand of her wit" or lived in hopeful ignorance of her desertion.

The suggestion in scene i of Husband's earlier desertion of another girl, although reported in the tract and fully elaborated in Wilkins' *Miseries of Enforced Marriage*, introduces a theme which seems to contradict the motivation for his rioting in the subsequent scenes of *A Yorkshire Tragedy*. In the tract Calverley's prodigality and depression are explained as God's revenge for his desertion of one to whom he had vowed marriage; in the *Miseries*, having been forced by his guardian to break his previous vow and to marry one of his guardian's choice, young Scarborow embraces a life of riot and dissipation in an effort to drown his sorrows. In *A Yorkshire Tragedy* it is only in scene i that the desertion of another girl is hinted at, and nowhere in the play is there the least suggestion of coercion or even that his marriage had taken place during his minority. Husband never expresses regret or remorse for not having married another; he confesses that it was "for fashion sake I married" (ii, 78), and inveighing against all marriages, curses "the very howre I *chose* a wife" (ii, 107). Without the explanation of the rioting as given in the tract or the excellent motivation that appears in the *Miseries*, *A Yorkshire Tragedy* follows much more closely the conventional portrayal of the Prodigal Son, presenting Husband merely as the typical prodigal, one who seeks a wife's dowry "to give new life Unto those pleasures which I most affect" (ii, 94), refuses a place at court with "Shall I that Dedicated my selfe to pleasure, be nowe confind in service" (iii, 57), and later realizes that he has been "Zany to a swine, to show tricks in the mire" (iv, 76–77).

And finally, as will, I think, be clear from the summary

given below, scenes ii–x of the *Tragedy* are in every way
complete in themselves—neither in agreement with what
is presented in scene i nor needing any introductory exposition.

A Yorkshire Tragedy

Scene ii. After Wife laments how Husband has consumed his credit in "Dice, and voluptuous meetings," Husband enters, curses his luck at dice, and, in reply to Wife's
question, blames her as the cause of his discontent. Wife,
again alone, observes how "much unlike Him selfe at first"
he is. Re-entering, Husband curses marriage because his
children must be beggars or knaves for want of wealth.
When Wife asks again the true cause of his discontent, he
replies "Mony, mony, mony, and thou must supply me";
though he married her for fashion's sake, he never could
abide her; her words shall not kill his pleasures; he will
hold her in contempt, be divorced from her bed "till thou
consent Thy dowry shall be sold to giue new life Vnto
those pleasures which I most affect." She promises and
leaves. He: "I hate the very howre I chose a wife: a trouble, trouble!" As he calls his wife strumpet and his children bastards, three gentlemen pass over stage and in turn
reprove him. A servant enters to say that Wife's uncle,
"your worships late guardian," had sent for her, and that
she has gone.

A gentleman enters: "I am come with confidence to
chide you." He preaches to Husband, naming his vices.
They fight, and as Husband lies wounded, Gentleman gives
further admonition. Husband, unrepentant, says 'tis lack
of money makes him weak.

Scene iii. Wife, returned from the visit to her uncle, tells Servant that, though her uncle knows of her husband's riots and debts, he thinks him kind to Wife and blames his riots on his youth; he will, therefore, prefer him to a place at court. She expects this to save her lands and free her husband from usurers. Husband enters demanding the money. When told of her uncle's promise, he demands, "Shall I that Dedicated my selfe to pleasure, be nowe confind in seruice to crouch and stand like an old man ith hams, my hat off? . . . Money, whore, money, or Ile —" and he draws his dagger. A servant interrupts to announce one from the university. Husband leaves and Wife in soliloquy laments her "miseries" and grief.

Scene iv. The Master of the College admonishes Husband for his riots and especially for allowing his brother, "the towardest hope of all our vniuersitie," to be seized on the bond he had signed for him.

Thanking Master for his words and pains, Husband orders wine, and after they have drunk, asks Master to walk about the grounds while he furnishes himself to relieve his brother. Alone, Husband, tearing at his hair, condemns himself for wasting his estate. His son entering, Husband stabs him that he may not live to be a beggar and carries the boy out to find his brother.

Scene v. A maid with the second child in her arms (as Wife sleeps) laments he will have no better fortune, "Tis lost at Dice what ancient honour won." Entering *"with the* [elder] *boie bleeding,"* Husband struggles with the maid for the second child. Wife, awaking, catches up the child, who in her arms is stabbed by Husband. She, hurt, sinks down. Husband knocks down a servant who would interfere and leaves to kill "my brat at nurse."

Scene vi. Meeting the Master of the College, who comments on his "distracted colour," Husband assures him it is but his fancy, and inviting him in, says he wants only one small part to make up the sum necessary to free his brother.

Scene vii. The servant, badly bruised and torn by Husband's spurs, says Husband had been "A man before of easie constitution Till now hells power supplied, to his soules wrong. Oh, how damnation can make weake men strong." Master, entering with two servants, sees the bloody sight: "has he somde vp theis To satisfie his brother?" As the wife regains consciousness, the wounded servant reports that Husband has gone to murder his child at nurse. Master leaves to stop him. Wife is led within where a surgeon waits.

Scene viii. Husband stumbles in, thrown by his horse, and before he can return to his horse to continue with his plan to "dispatch that little beggar," Master and three gentlemen seize him. As they will take him to the Justices, where "shall his deeds be blazd," he replies "Why, all the better. My glory tis to haue my action knowne: I grieue for nothing, but I mist of one."

Scene ix. A knight having expressed sorrow that ever Husband "took life and naturall being From such an honoured stock," Husband is brought in by Master "and the rest." He says: "I have consumd all, plaid awaie long acre, and I thought it the charitablest deed I could doe to cussen beggery and knock my house oth head." Repenting only that one is left unkilled, Husband is taken to gaol at Knight's order.

Scene x. Husband, led past his house on the way to gaol, asks to speak to his wife, who is "brought in a chaire." She is forgiving and he thoroughly repentant: "now glides the deuill from mee." Seeing his *"Children laid out,"* he wishes they might live "Though I did begge with you, which thing I feard." He hopes they, with angels, will pray for him. As officers would take him out: "Ile kisse the bloud I spilt and then I goe";

> Let euery father looke into my deedes,
> And then their heirs may prosper, while mine bleeds.

Master comforts Wife by noting that "one ioy is yet vn-murdered." She promises to sue for Husband's life and number all her friends to plead his pardon.

So unrelated to what follows is scene i of *A Yorkshire Tragedy* that one can hardly escape the conviction that it was added at some time after the other scenes had been written, for there is not the slightest basis for a suspicion that there once existed other scenes, now dropped, which presented a second plot, whether the story of the rejected girl or any other story. The single-minded purpose of the dramatist is revealed in the accuracy and completeness with which he presented only the material of the tract and, after the point at which he began, all the material of the tract. Yet it is difficult to understand why scene i should ever have been thought necessary. It could hardly have been to provide a part for a company comedian, for even the largest of the three servants' parts is very slight indeed. Mr. Marc Friedlaender, who argued convincingly that scene i was a late addition, offered the ingenious suggestion that it represented a brilliant effort—by Shakespeare—to render allowable a play, which without it would have been unallowable, by localizing all the subsequent action in London. Although he recognized that "the dis-

guise was apparent, and was meant to be," that all "who
went to the Globe to see the play knew the story well
enough to recognise the Calverley theme," he maintained
that "Neither the Cobhams nor the Calverleys could take
offence at a play which . . . had for its subject the murder of two of his children by an unnamed man in London." [6]

But the scenes which follow are certainly not localized in
London. As in the *Two Unnatural Murthers*, the tragedy
is enacted at Husband's ancestral home, i.e., Calverley
Hall. As he is conducted to the magistrate for examination,
Husband opens scene x by saying "I am right against my
house, seat of my ancestors"; and in the first scene of the
play proper (scene ii) he is advised that his wife, presumably on her way to sell her jewels, "was met by the way,
by them who were sent for her vp to London by her honorable vnkle (lines 125–26)." In modern idiom this statement is perhaps ambiguous, but the language is that of
the tract, where the context makes the meaning quite clear:
"Mistress *Cauerley*, going forward with this intent to sell
away her dowrie, was sent for vp to London by that honourable friend whose neece she was . . . who . . . at her
coming vp, began to question her . . . (p. 9) . . . hauing taken leaue of her honourable kinsman, she returned
toward *Cauerley*" (p. 10).

If, however, scene i fails to disguise the participants in
the tragedy by localizing the subsequent scenes in London,
for what purpose or reason was it added? If one must haz-
ard a suggestion, the most reasonable would seem to be
that scene i was added to encourage a resemblance between
A Yorkshire Tragedy and the *Miseries of Enforced Marriage*—that because one familiar with the latter play (and

they were both acted by the same company) recognized
that the *Tragedy*, in not presenting the history of Husband's earlier career, seemed by comparison to be lacking
sufficient motivation. That scene i was written with the
Miseries in mind seems borne out by the fact that Husband's rioting and mistreatment of his wife are in that
scene reported as "newes from London," while the entire action of the play is clearly in Yorkshire. In Wilkins'
play, on the contrary, young Scarborow (Calverley), de-
serting his wife, goes to London to erase his memories by
dissipation, and there the greater part of the play is laid
—all of it which coincides in time with the action presented
in *A Yorkshire Tragedy*. The news of Scarborow's marriage
to another in the *Miseries* is brought to Yorkshire by a
clown who enters with

> From London am I come, tho not with pipe and Drum,
> Yet I bring matter, in this poore paper,
> Will make my young mistris, delighting in kisses,
> Do as all Maidens will, hearing of such an ill,
> As to haue lost the thing they wisht most,
> A Husband, a Husband, a pretty sweet Husband,
> Cry oh, oh, oh, and alas. (C3v)

In both plays, then, a clown brings "from London" news
which will make cry out or go mad one who, again in both
plays, is identified as "my young mistress."

The full extent to which this opening scene of *A Yorkshire Tragedy* fails to accord with the rest of the tragedy
has often been misjudged because critics, recognizing obvious similarities between that play and *Miseries of Enforced Marriage*, have assumed the relationship of the two
plays to be closer than it is and have, indeed, tended to

assume that the latter play is little more than a revision of
the tragedy—a revision thought necessary because of the
prominence of the persons involved in the Calverleys'
tragedy. A summary of the *Miseries* reveals the changed
treatment:

Miseries of Enforced Marriage

Scene i. Young Scarborow, with gallants from the city,
in Yorkshire becomes betrothed to Clare, daughter of Sir
John Harcop, but immediately thereafter receives an order from his guardian to return to London.

Scene ii. In London his guardian, Lord Falconbridge,
tells Scarborow's uncle of his plan to marry Scarborow to
his niece; to forward the marriage he has brought Dr.
Baxter, Chancellor of Oxford. Scarborow returns and, advised of the plan for him, tells of his love for Clare.
Guardian, angry, orders his secretary to write a letter to
Sir John Harcop; the law permits a guardian to ruin a
disobedient ward, and he orders his steward to do just that.

Scene iii. Scarborow's earlier companions, Sir Francis
Ilford (a cheating gallant) and Wentloe, hearing that
Scarborow is married and melancholy, plan to win him
by mirth and undo him. Shortly after the melancholy Scarborow has joined them, the Clown enters with letters from
Sir John Harcop and Clare. Scarborow sends word to Clare
that he is married. He and his wife will go to his lands in
Yorkshire; Sir Francis Ilford and Wentloe will go along
to prey on him, now that he is rich.

Scene iv. Scarborow's younger brothers, Thomas from
the Inns of Court and John from Oxford, arrive at Sir
John Harcop's, the former, so he says, "to borrow money."

The clown arrives from London with Scarborow's letter to Clare announcing his marriage. As the others wait dinner for her, she reads and rereads the letter, then dies of a broken heart. Scarborow enters with Ilford, Wentloe, and his wife Katherine. He carries off the body of Clare, and his brother John reports to Katherine that Scarborow will have none of her, but has returned to London to drown his sorrow in dissipation.

Scene v. In London Ilford, Wentloe, and Bartley cheat Scarborow by arranging with a usurer to whom Ilford is in debt to come with sergeants and, doubling the debt owed him, persuade Scarborow to pay it. Scarborow, in aside, speaks of how clearly he sees his and his friends' evil life.

Scene vi. Thomas and John come to London from Yorkshire, seeking aid from their brother, but he rebukes them with Ilford's support. All draw swords and fight. Butler enters, takes no part in the fight, contrasts his old master with his new, and reports Scarborow the father of twin sons.

Scene vii. Enter John and Thomas, hurt, with their sister. After they have complained of their brother, Butler enters wounded by Scarborow when he had reported the birth of Scarborow's sons. He says he has a plan whereby the sister can live honest.

Scene viii. Scarborow, drunk and accompanied by Ilford, Wentloe, Bartley and Torchbearer, meets first Lord Falconbridge and then his uncle, Sir William Scarborow. He insults them and leaves. They remain to speak of his degradation but indicate they will try to help him.

Scene ix. Butler and Thomas and John Scarborow enter with loot, having robbed, as they afterwards discover, Sir John Harcop and his man of £300. Butler makes the brothers lie behind a hedge as he himself climbs a tree, and when Harcop enters, Butler persuades him that he had climbed the tree to learn which way the robbers went. The pursuit having taken the direction he indicated, Butler, giving money to the brothers, warns them against the practice of robbing.

Scene x. To help his master's sons and daughter, Butler tells Ilford, Wentloe, and Bartley of honest and rich wives he can get for them, and arranges for the latter two to meet him at a place where he apparently takes Ilford. Offstage he has arranged for Ilford to talk with Scarborow's sister, though her identity is not told him. He is made to overhear talk of her great wealth by her two brothers, whom Ilford thinks her uncles. Having quickly wed and bed her, he asks for her bonds, etc., only to learn that she is sister to bankrupt Scarborow. Wentloe and Bartley scoff at him. Discarding his new wife, Ilford goes off with his friends. Thomas and John return, curse their brother as cause of their misery. Vowing vengeance, Thomas leaves, while John follows to prevent his killing brother William.

Scene xi. After Scarborow soliloquizes on his prodigality, Thomas enters and would fight with him. Though Scarborow is at first unwilling, they are just beginning to fight when Ilford, Wentloe, and Bartley attack Scarborow. Thomas joins his brother in driving them out. Thomas would then slay his brother, but John enters to prevent him, and Thomas angrily leaves, saying that he will get John hanged by reporting to Sir John Harcop who it was that had robbed him. Scarborow suffers some from conscience, but when Butler brings in Katherine and the two children, Scarborow calls her strumpet, them bastards. To John, who enters, Butler promises to stay Thomas' trip to Sir John Harcop.

Scene xii. After Scarborow further rails upon his wife and Butler, Dr. Baxter of Oxford is brought in; he would preach at Scarborow, but the latter blames him for having knowingly married him to one he knew he did not love. Scarborow is prevented by Butler from killing wife, children, and Dr. Baxter. At the end the brothers are united; Ilford and his bride and Sir William enter; all is forgiven, and Sir William announces that Scarborow's guardian, realizing that he was to blame, had before his death given Scarborow double the wealth he had had.

Despite the differences in the endings of the two plays, the duration of the period in which husband and wife lived together, and the number of their children, it is at once obvious that *Miseries of Enforced Marriage* was in part based upon the Calverley murders.

The brief accounts which have been written of Walter Calverley's career prior to his murder of his sons have been quite inaccurate. He has been properly identified as the son and heir of William Calverley by his wife Katherine (daughter of John Thorneholme of Haysthorpe, Yorkshire), the eldest of eight brothers, the second, third, and fourth of whom were William, Thomas, and John. The Calverleys had been lords of the manors of Calverley and Pudsey, Yorkshire, since the twelfth century, and upon the death of his father Walter, still in his nonage, inherited as well lands at Burley-in-Wharfdale, Bagley, Farsley, Eccleshall, Bolton, and Seacroft. From that point in his career until the murders were committed, except for the name of his wife and children, what has been written of

Walter Calverley would appear to be pure fiction, or, at best, guesses based upon the two plays under discussion and the tract published in 1605—chiefly, it would seem, upon Wilkins' *Miseries of Enforced Marriage*. In the longest and most often consulted biographical sketch, that by Sir Sidney Lee in the *Dictionary of National Biography*, he is said to have been educated at Cambridge and is identified as the Walter Calverley who "entered as scholar of Clare Hall on 5 May 1579 and was matriculated on 1 Oct. following." In Venn's *Alumni Cantabrigienses* (1922) not only is this Walter Calverley identified as the murderer of his children but William Calverley, also of Clare Hall, B.A. 1581/2 and M.A. 1585, is declared to have been the brother who suffered imprisonment as a result of having been Walter's surety.[7] Neither of these identifications can be correct, for in May 1579, the date he is said to have entered Clare Hall, Walter Calverley the murderer was only one month old, his brother William yet unborn.[8] The Calverley family in Yorkshire was large, and William and Walter were frequent names in each generation. If, as the tract and both plays state, the younger brother of the murderer was at a university at the time of the murders, it must have been the William Calverley who was matriculated as pensioner from Trinity, Cambridge, Easter, 1604, home and parents unstated. There is no record of a Walter Calverley at either Oxford or Cambridge during the years he might have been expected to be a student, and as his parents were openly professed Catholics, it may be unlikely that Walter entered either university.[9]

Sir Sidney Lee, following earlier accounts, stated that after the death of William Calverley, Walter's father, who was buried 2 October 1596, "a relative of Lord Cobham became Calverley's guardian," and Walter "being left to his own devices at home in Yorkshire, affianced himself to the daughter of a humble neighbour. Subsequently coming to London, his guardian insisted on his breaking this engagement and on his marrying Philippa, daughter of Sir John Brooke, son of George, Lord Cobham. This marriage took place and proved Calverley's ruin. He withdrew to Calverley Hall with his wife, whom he detested, and sought distraction in drinking and gambling . . ."

All of this is, of course, close to what we are told in *Miseries of Enforced Marriage*, where, as in *Two Unnatural Murthers*, he was said to have been previously betrothed to a young woman of his own county and where, as in both *Two Unnatural Murthers* and *A Yorkshire Tragedy*, his guardian is said to have been an uncle of his wife.

There are, however, among the manuscripts preserved at Hatfield House a number of letters, hitherto neglected in this connection, which make it clear that the facts were quite different, that Walter's wife, Philippa Brooke, was rather the daughter of Sir Henry Cobham,[10] the diplomatist, who, though the fifth son of George Brooke, Lord Cobham, is always known by the surname Cobham.[11] Sir Henry had married Anne, daughter of Sir Henry Sutton of Nottinghamshire and widow of Walter Haddon, Master of Requests. Sir Robert Cecil, who had himself married a granddaughter of George Lord Cobham, received from Anne Lady Cobham a goodly number of letters, some of them addressed "To my verie hon-

orable good nephew" and nearly all of them concerned
with furthering the fortunes of her sons or with arranging
advantageous marriages for her daughters.

After having the year before enlisted Cecil's aid in advancing the marriage of her eldest daughter to the eldest
son of Sergeant Heron, Lady Cobham wrote him again
on 30 May 1599 with reference to a proposed marriage of
her younger daughter Philippa.

There is a marriage intended between my daughter Phillipe and
Mr. Coverley, of Coverley; and for that I am loth to deal in so
weighty a cause without my Lord Cobham's advice and yours, I
have thought good to send Mr. Lyly to you, who can declare all
his estate to you. Likewise I have sent another gentleman unto
my Lord Cobham to desire him to impart it unto you. I beseech
you (who hath been always a father to my children) that you will
so deal with Mr. Lyly that if you find it fit it may be brought to
pass (which gentleman is kin to Mr. Lyly's wife, who is the first
well-wisher of this match towards my daughter). I understand
by Mr. Lyly that he is in Wardship till April next to the Lady
Gargrave, of Yorkshire, who hath tendered unto him her daughter, and is willing to give £1,500 in marriage with her. But he
hath taken some liking of my daughter, that he is content to take
her with a lesser portion.—From Durham House, this 30 May
'99.[12]

From this letter it would appear that the conventional
retelling of the story of Walter Calverley should be corrected in several respects. The date of his birth is set as
April 1579; his wife Philippa was the daughter not of
Sir John Brooke but of Sir Henry Cobham and his wife
Anne Lady Cobham; and clearly at the time the marriage
was first discussed Calverley's guardian was not "a rela-

tive of Lord Cobham" but Lady Gargrave of Yorkshire, of whose position Lady Cobham apparently knew only after she had been informed by Mr. Lyly. That the information given by Mr. Lyly was correct is proved by the action taken by the court at York in Curia Wardorum et liberacionum on 23 June 1598, which declared that

Whereas the custodye wardshipp & marriage of Walter Calverley her Maiesties Warde sonne and heyer of William Calverley esquier decessed by Indenture bering date the xxvth day of Marche anno xxxix^a Dicte Domine Regine and also the lese of the said Wardes landes by another Indenture dated the first day of Aprill in the said xxxixth yere of our said soueraign lady, are graunted unto Katheryn Calverley widow and William Calverley gent. . . . Now this day uppon the sute of the said Katheryn & William for licence that they might sett over their estate & interest in the said wardshipp & marriage and also in the said lese unto Anne lady gargrave late wief of Sir Cotton gargraue knight decessed & to Richard gargrave esquier her sonne. Lycence is graunted unto them the said Katheryn & William Calverley to alyen assigne & sett over the aforesaid severall Indentures and all their interest right & title in the custody wardship & mariage of the said Walter Calverley & in the lese of his landes unto the said lady Gargrave & Richard gargrave . . .[13]

Both Lady Gargrave and her son survived Walter Calverley by thirty years or more.

Further, if we can accept Lady Cobham as an impartial witness, young Calverley, far from being forced into a marriage with a niece of his guardian, successfully withstood his guardian's effort to marry him to her own daughter, preferring marriage with Philippa even though it meant the sacrifice of a substantial dowry. Unless we assume that

the deserted girl of the later accounts was not the daughter
of Lady Gargrave [14] but still another young woman in
Yorkshire to whom he had contracted himself, it would
appear that Calverley married according to his liking.
Whether or not either Cecil or Lord Cobham, to effect the
marriage of Calverley to their kinswoman, exerted pres-
sure upon Lady Gargrave or her ward, Walter and Philippa were married within the year.

Lady Cobham again wrote her kinsman Cecil on 20
April 1600, asking that he "peruse this enclosed petition
preferred in behalf of Mr. Calverley (an 'unstayed' young
man) her Majesty's ward, who hath married my daughter. According to the petition, I desire your favour and
furtherance therein." [15] The nature of the enclosed petition remains secret, for the petition itself does not survive;
nor is there any record of whether Cecil undertook to
further it. It may, perhaps, be to favorable action on this
petition that both *Two Unnatural Murthers* and *A Yorkshire Tragedy* refer when stating that Calverley's wife's
uncle arranged for him a place at court. Lady Cobham,
it may be remarked, seems already to be somewhat out of
patience with the " 'unstayed' young man," her new son-
in-law.

One other letter among the Cecil papers concerns Walter Calverley. It is, again, a letter to Sir Robert from Lady
Cobham, written two months from the day on which she
presumably sought some sort of preferment for young
Calverley. In this letter she shows clearly that her interest
in the marriage had been solely and coldly financial. She
reminds Sir Robert that she had "married her daughter
to Walter Calverley, who by reason of minority was unable to make her any jointure. He is now imprisoned in

the Fleet on an execution, and his life is much doubted." Lady Cobham asks no help for the husband of her unfortunate daughter; she merely prays that "If he should die . . . the wardship of his brother may be bestowed on her daughter." [16]

Sir Robert Cecil continued to receive letters from Lady Cobham, but in those that survive there is no other mention of Walter or Philippa Calverley; the remaining letters concern only preferment for her sons John and Calisthenes, or request Cecil's influence in securing a knighthood for her son-in-law, the son of Sergeant Heron.

We cannot say how long Walter Calverley remained in the Fleet or how he gained his freedom. It is possible that other members of his wife's family came to his assistance, for they seem shortly thereafter to have taken steps to conserve the Calverley estates. In the Trinity term, 44 Elizabeth, John Brooke, Kt., and Edward Heron, presumably the husband of Philippa's elder sister, are among the four plaintiffs against Walter Calverley and his wife Philippa, deforciants, with reference to "manors in Calverley and Pudsey . . . with lands in the same and in Ecclesell, Farseley, and Woodall." [17]

As a result of this action, in "A° 44 Eliz. the manors of Calverley and Pudsey, with the appurtenances in Calverley, Eccleshall, Farseley, Woodhall, and Pudsey, were vested in trust on Sir John Brooke and others for and during the joint natural lives of Walter Calverley, Esq. and Philippa his wife, and after their decease to the use and behoof of William Calverley, son and heir apparent, and his heirs male." [18] Although this action may perhaps have been in part inaugurated because of the reckless life being led by young Calverley, the principal rea-

son for the trusteeship was presumably that the lands were
subject to confiscation, Walter being, like his parents, a
recognized Catholic. It would appear not unlikely that it
was this appointment of Sir John Brooke as a trustee of
the Calverley lands, shortly after Walter became of age
and more than two years after his marriage, that led to the
belief that a kinsman of his wife had been Calverley's
guardian during his minority.

Lady Cobham's three surviving letters concerning Walter Calverley, which seem so clearly to foreshadow the
tragedy on St. George's Day, 1605, suggest the manner in
which, after the horror of the succeeding events, his story
was embellished, perhaps by repeated oral transmission,
perhaps by conscious "literary" additions.

The Calverley Register, although it contains no reference
to the baptism of Walter's eldest son, William, records the
baptism of the second son, Walter, on 4 October 1603 and
that of the youngest son, Henry, on 10 October 1604. On
St. George's Day 1605, therefore, the infant out at nurse
was slightly more than six months old, the child stabbed
in his mother's arms a year older, and the eldest son, in
the tragedy appealingly presented with his top, could not
have been more than five.

The final record in the tragedy—other than Calverley's
execution the following August—is his examination before
the justices of the peace, Sir John Saville and Sir Thomas
Bland, on the day following the murders. This is reprinted,
as it too suggests the literary embellishment the story
underwent.

Being examined whether he did kill two of his own children . . .
[Calverley] saith, that he did kill them both at his owne house at
Calverley yesterday, being the 23rd day of April . . . Being

further examined what moved him to wound his wife yesterday, to that he said, that one Carver coming into the chamber where he was with his said wife, he commanded her to will the said Carver to goe and fetch another son of his, whose name is Henry Calverley, who was nursed by the said Carvers wife, which she accordingly did; whereupon the said Carver went downe into the court, and stayed there about a quarter of an houre, and returned again, but brought not the said child with him; and being commanded to go downe again, he refused so to doe, and that therefore he did wound his wife, if she be wounded. And being further examined, what he wold have don to the said childe if Carver had brought him, to that he said he wold have killed him also. And being likewise examined whether at any time he had any intention to kill his said children, to that he said, that he hath had an intention to kill them for the whole space of two years past, and the reasons that moved him thereunto was, for that his said wife had many times theretofore uttered speeches and given signes and tokens unto him, whereby he might easily percieve and conjecture, that the said children were not by him begotten, and that he hath found himselfe to be in danger of his life sundry times by his wife.[19]

It would perhaps be unwise to assume that at this examination Walter Calverley gave correctly and in full the reasons for his actions, or that all which appears in the later accounts is, if unmentioned by him, literary embellishment. There may well have been some reason for his failing to mention the imprisonment of his brother and the visit by the Master of the College. If he were indeed convinced that his wife's children were not by him, he may have omitted reference to his brother in his examination for the same reason that, Whitaker suggested, he stood mute at his trial, not to protect his heirs, for the estate, being in strict settlement, would not have been affected by a forfeiture, but rather to benefit his brother by making it possible for his creditors to be satisfied. It may well have been that the report concerning his brother decided him to put into execution at once the thought which he had entertained "for the whole space of two years" of killing the children, whose legitimacy he questioned, and so make his imprisoned brother his heir.

However that may be, there are in all three of the later accounts a number of additions which seem clearly to be conscious literary embellishments. Although in the later accounts Calverley (or Husband or Scarborow) repeatedly calls his children bastards and his wife whore, and charges another with being her lover, the impression given is that his doing so is not an expression of his true convictions but rather a desire to torture and an indication of the degradation into which he has fallen. In the later accounts it is the husband's realization of the cost of his prodigality and his fear that his children must become beggars—not his belief in their illegitimacy—that prompts his decision that they must die. It is this change which makes possible in the later accounts the tearful reconciliation of husband and wife, the happy ending of the *Miseries* and, in the tract and *A Yorkshire Tragedy*, the husband's remorseful wish that his children were alive again, even if he begged with them.

Another addition common to all three of the extant literary accounts is, as has been noted, the identification of his wife's uncle as Walter Calverley's guardian—an identification which is clearly incorrect unless Lady Gargrave, refusing to give her consent to her ward's marriage to one other than her daughter, was, through the influence of either

Cecil or Cobham, replaced by one of their own kinsmen. In the records, however, no such change of guardians has come to light; nor does it seem likely that two such prominent ministers of the queen should have been forced to such an expediency.

The author of *A Yorkshire Tragedy*, following in every detail the tract, his source, is himself responsible for no embellishment of the story; and possibly the conscious literary embellishments introduced by Wilkins are limited to the changes made necessary by his substitution of a happy ending and by his theme of enforced marriage. Although it seems certain that he made use of *Two Unnatural Murthers* and *A Yorkshire Tragedy*, Wilkins seems clearly to have possessed certain knowledge of the Calverley incident not supplied by them—knowledge acquired perhaps from rumor or by his own investigation. Although Lady Cobham's testimony that Calverley sought marriage with Philippa is supported by both *Two Unnatural Murthers* and *A Yorkshire Tragedy*, in neither of which is there the slightest suggestion of coercion, later rumors may well have sought to explain Calverley's brutal behavior by reporting that he had been forced into his marriage. Other more specific details introduced by Wilkins show that he possessed information about the Calverleys which he could not have got from the earlier accounts. For instance, neither of them cites a specific age for Walter at any point in the narrative; Wilkins, on the other hand, is quite specific and surprisingly accurate. William Scarborow at the opening of the play will be "Eighteene . . . next Pentecost" (B2); Walter Calverley was eighteen the April following the death of his father in October. Later in the play (I4) William is "three and twenty"; Walter had just com-

pleted his twenty-fifth year when he killed his sons. Much
more surprisingly, however, although changing the family
name from Calverley to Scarborow, Wilkins assigns Walter Caverley and his wife Philippa the names William and
Katherine, which, interestingly, were the names of the
murderer's parents, and he correctly calls two of his
brothers John and Thomas.[20] As chance could hardly account for the appearance of these four names, it seems
probable that Wilkins had another source for some of his
details. That source could, of course, have been merely
oral report—perhaps confused oral report, as is suggested
by his calling the murderer William rather than Walter.
It is remarkable that the murderer, although correctly
identified as Walter Calverley in the 1607 edition of
Stow's *Chronicles*, is in E. Howes' *Abridgement* of 1611
called William Calverley.[21] Unless, as seems most unlikely, the reviser of the chronicle entry changed the name
because of his recollection of Wilkins' play, there would
seem to have been current an account of the Calverley
murders, known to both Howes and Wilkins, in which the
murderer was confused with his father William Calverley,
husband of Katherine. Such a confusion may perhaps have
been encouraged by the prompt efforts made in Chancery
by Philippa, "widow of Walter Calverley, deceased," to
have her surviving infant son Henry relieved of the fines
which, during many years before his death in 1596,
William, his grandfather, had incurred by absenting himself from church. The discharge to Henry Calverley on
28 December 1605 of the fines levied against William
Calverley is fully recorded in Patent Roll (Chancery) 3
James I, Part 9 (C 66/1671). This discharge, if talked
about at all, may well have left with many the impression

that Henry was being relieved of the debts of his father, whose story had so recently been a subject of interest. But whether or not Wilkins did indeed confuse Walter with his father William, it is clear that he knew more of the family than he could have found in either *A Yorkshire Tragedy* as we have it, where no names appear, or the *Two Unnatural Murthers*, where none but Walter's is given. Further, it is clear that he made only the most half-hearted effort to disguise the identity of the unfortunate family—an effort which extended no further than the substitution of the family name Scarborow for that of Calverley; that is, the substitution of the name of one old Yorkshire town for that of another.

I have found it expedient in several instances to refer to "*A Yorkshire Tragedy* as we have it." Such qualifications seemed advisable until there was an opportunity for further discussion of the theory that the *Tragedy* as it has come down to us represents not what was presented on the stage, but a revision made some years after the original play had been written. On the first page of the quarto, it will be remembered, *A Yorkshire Tragedy* is further identified as "All's One, or, One of the Foure Plaies in One, called A York-shire Tragedy." Its length, between 700 and 800 lines, justifies the belief that it must have been acted with three other plays of approximately the same length, the performance of the four requiring a time roughly equivalent to that of the usual five-act play. A theory first suggested by Fleay and later developed by Mr. H. Dugdale Sykes[22] holds (1) that the reference in scene i to the "young mistress" (the Clare Harcop of *The Miseries*) is "in itself sufficient proof that the proper construction to be put upon the title *All's One, or one of the Four Plays in One, called A York-*

shire Tragedy is that the *Tragedy* was one of four plays
all dealing with the history of Walter Calverley, the reference to the 'young mistress' being a reference to a character appearing in one of the three other plays"; (2) that
"the obviously unpremeditated [23] conclusion of *The Miseries* and the subsequent appearance of *A Yorkshire Tragedy* with its nameless *dramatis personae* suggest that in the
Tragedy we have the original tragic ending of *The Miseries"*; (3) that, the *Four Plays in One* having been inhibited
as being offensive to the susceptibilities of Calverley's relations, Wilkins, in order to render the play more acceptable, "disguised its references to Calverley by introducing
throughout a large admixture of romance, giving fictitious
names to the personages of the story, discarding the final
scenes" of the original and substituting the scene of reconciliation; and (4) that later "the prohibition of the repre-
sentation of the actual facts of the crime having been withdrawn, the discarded portion of *The Miseries* was . . .
published as *A Yorkshire Tragedy,* with the names of the
characters suppressed."

In regard to point 1, I can see nothing to support the
view that all of the *Four Plays in One* must have been
concerned with the career of Walter Calverley, much to
discredit it. Why should his career have been divided into
four separate and distinct plays if, as "Four Plays in One"
certainly indicates, they were designed to be performed together? Aside from the story of the deserted girl, what
could the other plays have dealt with? Nothing else is
suggested in the tract which the surviving play follows
in such detail. The several plots of the *Miseries* could
hardly have been so separated as to be told each independently in another of the plays. Except for the vague sug-

gestion of a deserted girl in scene i, there is in the *Tragedy*
no reference to events in Calverley's earlier life, nothing
to suggest that the audience had previously witnessed on
the stage him, his brothers, or his sister. Indeed, the
literal way in which the author of *A Yorkshire Tragedy*
confined himself strictly to the tract, introducing nothing
not there found, strongly urges that he wrote the tragedy
as a piece complete in itself.

The title-page cites only the title *A Yorkshire Tragedy*.
The reading above the first page of text, "All's One, or,
one of the foure plaies in one, called A York-shire Tragedy," must, I believe, be interpreted as an effort to indicate that one of the four plays performed together was the
play which follows, i.e., *A Yorkshire Tragedy*. The usual
meaning of the words 'All's One,' as repeatedly used by
Shakespeare and others, was and is, of course, 'it makes no
difference.' Although it would seem most ill-chosen, *All's
One* would appear from the wording and the punctuation
to be an alternate title to *A Yorkshire Tragedy;* more
aptly it could have been the title of the four plays which
were intended to be acted together as the equivalent of
one five act play. Possibly all four plays were concerned
with one theme; but I can see no reason for believing that
the intended meaning of 'All's One' was that all four
dealt with the affairs of the same family.

Points 2 and 4 of Mr. Sykes's argument can be discussed together. Is there any evidence that when *A Yorkshire Tragedy* was published the original names of the
dramatis personae were suppressed? The only evidence for
such suppression which I see is that there is in the play
not only no reference to Calverley by name but none to
Yorkshire. The tragedy, as I have repeatedly noted, fol-

lows exactly the story as told in *Two Unnatural Murthers*; there is, therefore, no reason to believe that the dramatist knew anything about the Calverleys other than what he got from that account. In that account the wife's name is not given nor are the names of any others except that of Sir John Saville, before whom Calverley was brought after he had been captured—a very minor figure in both tract and play. All the others, Wife, Guardian, Nurse, Brother, Master of the College, a Gentleman, three gentlemen, servants and children are nameless in the tract and are identified by the same type designations in both tract and play. If in an earlier form of the play the characters bore other names, the exciser must have returned to the tract to find suitable designations for them—a most unlikely procedure. The suppression of names, therefore, could have extended no further than the dropping of the name Calverley, which may well not have appeared in an original draft. In many plays of the period are the characters no more specifically identified. One must remember that an acted play does not require a list of the dramatis personae, however helpful such a list may be when a play is read.

To Mr. Sykes's point 3 I should have two objections. First he argued that the *Miseries* could "represent a combination of the three other plays (in *Four Plays in One*), or parts of them, altered and rewritten to form a homogeneous whole . . . Even as it now stands it contains two entirely independent plots, the tragedy of the betrothal, betrayal, and death of Scarborow's (Calverley's) forsaken mistress, and the comedy of Ilford's unwitting marriage with the penniless sister of the man whom he had himself brought to ruin." Immediately afterwards Mr. Sykes urges that Wilkins, to render his play more acceptable, "dis-

guised its references to Calverley by introducing throughout a large admixture of romance, giving fictitious names
to the personages of the story." What is the large admixture of romance to which he refers? If the stories of Ilford
and Clare Harcop, romance though they be, were in the
Four Plays as Mr. Sykes envisages them, Wilkins obviously
did not add them to disguise the connection with Calverley.
Indeed, as I have pointed out, Wilkins, far from seeking
to becloud the connection with the Calverleys, actually
strengthened the connection, introducing what could not
have appeared in any form of the tragedy (since they do
not appear in its source), the actual Christian names of
the Calverley family. Further, had the family of Walter's
wife, the Brookes, exerted its influence toward the closure
of *A Yorkshire Tragedy*, it would hardly have been satisfied by the changes introduced into the *Miseries;* there, indeed, it would have found much more to object to. In
A Yorkshire Tragedy (as in *Two Unnatural Murthers*,
and therefore certainly in any earlier draft of the *Tragedy*)
the wife's uncle—and hence presumably a Brooke—does
not appear on stage but is reported as kindly, generous,
and forgiving (iii, 13–20); no mention is made, as in
the *Miseries*, of his having forced his ward into marriage
with his niece upon threat of ruining his estate even when
he knew of his ward's previous contract to marry another.
Save in scene i there is in *A Yorkshire Tragedy* no indication that Husband, when he married, deserted an earlier
love; never is it suggested that he had been denied the
right to marry whom he wished. As has been noted, he
speaks of when "I chose a wife." In the *Miseries*, on the
other hand, the sole responsibility for the death of Clare
Harcop and all the ensuing unhappiness resulting from

the enforced marriage is laid squarely upon the guardian,
identified as a member of the wife's family. Had the
Brookes objected to his role in *A Yorkshire Tragedy*,
they could hardly have been pleased by the change introduced into the *Miseries*.[24]

There is, I may note in passing, one very puzzling
feature in the part of the guardian as he appears in the
Miseries. In each of the three stage directions indicating
his entry he is referred to as Lord Faulconbridge (or
Falconbridge), and of the thirty-eight speeches assigned
to him, thirty-six are headed "Lord," "Lo," or "Lor."
His two remaining speeches, however, are headed
"Hunsd." (B2) and "Huns." (B4). As he is throughout
the play always addressed and spoken of merely as "My
Lord" or "guardian," no one hearing the play in the
theatre could know, or would be likely to ask, what his
lordship's title was. His name would be buried in the
playbook's stage directions until a publisher placed the
play in print. Inasmuch as his very first speech is headed
"Hunsd.," it might at first be thought that perhaps the
speech-heading indicated the actor who was to take the
part, but unfortunately none of the actors known to have
been members of the King's Men, by whom the title-page
declares the play to have been acted, bore a name which
could have been so abbreviated; nor do the incomplete
records of other companies reveal an actor with such a
name. Too, were "Hunsd." the abbreviation of the name of
an actor, one would expect it to appear not as a speech-heading but in the stage direction indicating his entry. It would
seem, therefore, that unless the compositor suffered a lapse
of some sort and twice substituted "Hunsd." (or "Huns.")
for "Lord," the title of the guardian must at some time

have been changed to Falconbridge—a safe change since the barony of Fauconberg (Falconbridge) had been in abeyance since the death of William Neville in 1463. If the "Hunsd." was intended as an abbreviation of an actual title, it could only have been for Lord Hunsdon—a designation we would expect to be promptly changed, for the title was held during Walter Calverley's minority by George Carey, second Lord Hunsdon, cousin and Lord Chamberlain to Queen Elizabeth and patron of the company which acted the play. Although by the time the play was written the title had passed to his brother John and the company had been accepted as the King's Men, it seems unlikely that the company would within three years of his death have presented their former patron in so unkind a manner.[25]

A change in the title given the guardian is, of course, no evidence that the *Miseries* underwent revision. Lord Hunsdon was not Walter Calverley's guardian, and as has been said, in the acted play the guardian has no name other than "Lord."

In dating *A Yorkshire Tragedy* and *Miseries of Enforced Marriage* scholars have tended to be conservative and to assign to them a date no earlier than 1606 for the tragedy and 1607 for *Miseries*. Aside from the entry of *Two Unnatural Murthers* on the Stationers' Register there is absolutely no clue to the date of *A Yorkshire Tragedy*, and for the dating of the *Miseries* the clues are only slightly less scarce. However, on the basis of an assumption which I think justified, and with no evidence to the contrary, it seems reasonably safe to urge the later part of 1605 as the date of the *Tragedy* and not later than the first five months of 1606 as that of the *Miseries*.

Although it was the second to be printed by almost a full year, *A Yorkshire Tragedy* must have been the earlier, as has indeed been generally recognized. That it was the earlier is urged by the treatment of the Calverley story in the two plays: the tragedy following with no variation whatsoever the events as related in *Two Unnatural Murthers*, even to the paraphrasing of a great many speeches, while in the *Miseries*, though its author appears to have had some information of the Calverleys not in the earlier accounts, the story is presented with such imaginative liberties as suggest that some little time at least had elapsed since Walter Calverley's frightful act had first shocked the country.

The tract on which the *Tragedy* was based, entered on the Stationers' Register on 12 June 1605, must have been for sale shortly thereafter. As an occasional pamphlet it would have been read promptly by those interested in the April murders or the August execution, and then largely neglected. That the *Tragedy*, too, may well have been hurried to completion in the hope of capitalizing on the horror which the story had aroused, is suggested not only by its brevity and the exactness with which it follows the tract in phrasing and step by step in the narrative, but perhaps even by its ending. Walter Calverley, having refused to plead, was pressed to death at York on 5 August 1605. *Two Unnatural Murthers*, having been printed prior to the execution, closes with mention of his remorse and his wife's continuing love for him, even after his cruelty. So too ends *A Yorkshire Tragedy*. Although the closing lines, spoken by Master,

> Two brothers: one in bond lies ouerthrowne,
> This on a deadlier execution,

may imply that Husband is to be put to death, the last speech of the wife, which immediately precedes it,

> Dearer than all is my poore husbands life:
> Heauen giue my body strength, which yet is faint
> With much expence of bloud, and I will kneele,
> Sue for his life, nomber vp all my friends,
> To plead for pardon [for] my deare husbands life,

suggests that the dramatist may have been writing before Calverley's execution, or at least in ignorance of it. Although such an abandonment of the story in suspense is obviously an effective and infinitely the more artistic ending, one may agree that few Elizabethan chroniclers, ever eager to underscore a moral, would have deliberately omitted the wages exacted for such crimes.

Doubtless the reason that the *Miseries* has been assigned to a date as late as 1607, the year of its publication, is that there has been assumed to be an allusion to *Don Quixote* in Scarborow's declaring "Now I am armd to fight with a Wind-mill" (F). Many references to *Don Quixote* in Spain in 1604 indicate that Cervantes' manuscript was widely circulated and acclaimed before its publication early in 1605. The first English translation of Cervantes' satire —or rather the first part of it, which contains the account of the knight's attack upon the windmills—was not published until 1612, but it had been made some years before and it, too, is presumed to have been circulated in manuscript. But Wilkins' allusion to the fight with the windmills is so vague and, indeed, so inexact as to suggest that he not only had never read the account in either Spanish or English but had a most imperfect conception of the incident as Cervantes relates it. The passage in Wilkins suggests none of the romantic innocence which leads Cer-

vantes' hero to mistake the windmills for giants; rather
it seems to mean little more than "I feel like doing something foolish," or "In my present state I don't care what
happens." The full speech, spoken by Scarborow as he,
drunk, enters with gallants and a Torchbearer, is:

Boy, beare the Torch faire: Nowe am I armd to fight with a
Wind-mill, and to take the wall of an Emperor: Much drink, no
money: A heauy head, and a light paire of heeles (F).

The suggestion of desperation in the words "Much
drink, no money" is more pronounced in a similar allusion
found in a passage in Middleton's *Your Five Gallants*,
which is, perhaps, even less reminiscent of the incident in
Don Quixote. There Pyamont, angered by the theft of his
gold, exclaims:

No less than forty pound of fair gold at one lift . . . Heart,
nothing vexes me so much, but that I paid the goldsmith for the
change too not an hour before: had I let it alone in a chaine of
silver as it was at first, it might have given me some notice of his
departure: 'sfoot, I could fight with a windwill now. (IV, viii)

These two passages are so similar in their phrasing, their
meaning, and their distortion of the situation found in
Don Quixote, that one seems clearly indebted to the other
—unless perhaps "Fight with a windmill" had so quickly
passed into London slang with a perverted connotation.

If one is indebted to the other, it appears more likely
that Middleton is the borrower, not so much because Wilkins' reference seems closer to the spirit of *Don Quixote*
(for "take the wall of an Emperor" here refers not to a
knightly and victorious deed but only to keeping the inner
side of the sidewalk and thereby forcing another into the

street), but rather because another passage in *Your Five Gallants* seems possibly to allude to the Calverley murders as recounted in the *Miseries*. When in the last scene of *Your Five Gallants* Fitzgrave forces the cheating gallants to take their punks as wives, Goldstone observes "These forc'd marriages do never come to good," and Pursenet adds "They often prove the ruin of great houses." The reference here is clearly not to *Two Unnatural Murthers* or to *A Yorkshire Tragedy*, for there is in them no suggestion of enforced marriage; nor does Pursenet's remark about "the ruin of great houses" exactly fit the *Miseries*, at the end of which young Scarborow, as the heir of his remorseful guardian, inherits greater wealth than he had had before entering upon his prodigality. Nonetheless, the inclusion in both plays, with distorted meaning, of a similarly phrased allusion to the same episode in *Don Quixote*, strongly suggests that Middleton, though altering the reference to agree with what he had elsewhere learned of the Calverley family, derived the original suggestion for the two gallants' remarks from Wilkins' *Miseries of Enforced Marriage*.

But Middleton's indebtedness, if such it be, offers little help in dating either *A Yorkshire Tragedy* or *Miseries of Enforced Marriage*, since *Your Five Gallants* can be no more definitely dated than sometime within the period from November 5, 1605, which is referred to as "a dismal day" (II, ii, 14), and its entry on the Stationers' Register 22 March 1607/8, more than seven months after the entry of Wilkins' play.

Yet *Miseries of Enforced Marriage* can, I believe, be more definitely dated, and, therefore, so can *A Yorkshire Tragedy* in that it seems clearly to precede *Miseries*. If the text which we have of the latter play represents that actually acted, it could hardly have appeared after May 1606, for with the proroguing of Parliament on the 27th of that month there became effective An Act to Restrain Abuses of Players, which provided that

if . . . after the end of this present Session of Parliament, any person or persons doe or shall in any Stage play . . . jestingly or prophanely speake or use the holy Name of God or of Christ Jesus, or of the Holy Ghoste or of the Trinitie, which are not to be spoken but with feare and reverence, [he or they] shall forfeite for everie such Offence by hym or them committed Tenne Pounds.[26]

Although when the *Miseries* was printed in 1607 the title-page claimed that the quarto presented it "As it is now playd by his Maiesties Seruants," the company could hardly have been so reckless then as to present the text of the play as printed. According to Sir Edmund Chambers, Sir George Buck, as deputy and successor to his uncle, Edmund Tilney, exercised the function of the Master of the Revels from 1603 on and, "presumably with this act in mind, excised such expletives as 'life' and 'heart,'" while in other instances "these and others, such as 'mass' and 'faith,' which one would have supposed to be as much or as little objectionable, remain unquestioned." [27] The oaths in the *Miseries*, however, are of a different and stronger sort—the very sort certainly which the Act sought to eradicate: "by Jesu" (A3v), "Gods precious" (C4v, D1v, G2v), "a Gods name" (G3), "Before God" (A3v), "A Gods sake" (A2, I v), "God of his goodness" (as an oath, A4v), "O God" (A3 twice, B, B3v, C4v), etc. Both *A Yorkshire*

Tragedy and, especially, the *Two Unnatural Murthers* are remarkably free from such oaths. In the *Miseries* the dramatist has consciously, it would seem, inserted them in abundance. "This statute," Sir Edmund Chambers noted, "even if not always literally observed, entailed much revision of existing dramatic texts." [28] It is hard to believe that, had the play-book been presented to him for his approval after May 1606, Buck would have permitted such expletives as "by Jesu" and "Gods precious" to stand. It would appear, therefore, either that the *Miseries* was presented prior to the enactment of the statute or that the text of the play that was printed was not the same as that approved by Buck and acted by the King's Men.

The evidence for dating the two plays is, as I have admitted, neither exact nor, perhaps, convincing, but such evidence as there is suggests that *A Yorkshire Tragedy* was written only a short time after the murders had been committed—possibly, like *Two Unnatural Murthers* and the ballad *Lamentable Murther Done in Yorkshire*, before news of Calverley's execution in August had reached London. In spite of its dramatic force, it is, with its naked horror, clearly an occasional piece written to take advantage of a momentary interest. As that interest might be expected to decline rapidly during the months following the execution, it would not be surprising should the actors have thought fit to substitute for it a version which treated the story with greater imaginative liberty and which, as a full five-act play, might be presented by itself, without the three other pieces which went to make up *Four Plays in One*, they too, perhaps, being of occasional and fugitive interest. Accordingly, the company may well have accepted or commissioned Wilkins' play during late 1605 or early 1606. The text of the *Miseries* as it has come down to us seems clearly to have been prepared before May 1606.

Few critics have failed to recognize the dramatic effectiveness of *A Yorkshire Tragedy*. Pope, to be sure, called it "a wretched play" and Halliwell-Phillipps pronounced it "an insignificant piece, of some little merit, but no dramatic power"; [29] at the time, however, they were most concerned that the play not be accepted as by William Shakespeare. To Sir A. W. Ward, even though he accepted Shakespeare's authorship of certain passages, the play seemed a "hasty" production "and one dependent in part upon claptrap." [30] Hastily written it probably was, but to most critics it is rather its freedom from claptrap (as it usually appears in Elizabethan tragedy), its bare realism, and its fierce dramatic power which distinguish *A Yorkshire Tragedy* and set it among the few truly great domestic tragedies of its age. Swinburne declared it full "to overflowing of fierce animal power, and hot as with the furious breath of some caged wild beast. . . . It is and must always be," he wrote, "unsurpassable for pure potency of horror; and the breathless heat of its action, its raging rate of speed, leaves actually no breathing-time for disgust; it consumes our very sense of repulsion as with fire. ' 'Tis a very excellent piece of work' " . . . [31]

We finish reading *A Yorkshire Tragedy*, wrote J. A. Symonds, "with the same kind of impression as that left upon our sight by a flash of lightning revealing some grim object in a night of pitchy darkness. The mental retina has been all but seared and blinded; yet the scene discovered in that second shall not be forgotten." [32] The most recent editor of the play, the late Tucker Brooke, declared: "The

barbaric force of the play and the splendour of some of
the prose it contains cannot fail to impress the reader." [33]
And the same effectiveness is recognized by a living critic,
who writes of it as "a truly great play," wherein "the crude
realism . . . is given something of a monumental tone by
[Husband's] villainy, repentance, and final series of ghastly
murders. There is an advance here on the characterization
of *Arden of Feversham,* and there seems, in spite of the
shortness of the piece, an attempt at securing some broader
and loftier appeal." [34]

The powerful effect created by the play on most readers
is, I suspect, due in large part to the play's brevity and to
the swiftness with which it reaches its climax, with no
comedy interspersed and without the distraction of a sub-
plot. The only attempt at comedy, and that but slight, is
to be found in the inharmonious scene i, the characters in
which do not, indeed could not, reappear in any later
scene. There are, moreover, some deeply thoughtful and
well-expressed speeches which have contributed to the once
widely accepted view that Shakespeare either was the author of the play or had some share in its composition. The
dramatist, whoever he was, obviously had a mature, even
an enquiring mind. Not content merely to relate what had
happened, as was the author of the tract, he sought to
answer the question why Husband had behaved as he had.
Husband himself is made to give the only possible explanation and to voice the prayer that the devil which had possessed him might be bound by

> . . . you blessed Angells,
> In that pit bottomlesse; let him not rise
> To make men act vnnaturall tragedies,
> To spred into a father, and in furie,

Make him his childrens executioners;
Murder his wife, his seruants, and who not?
For that man's darke, where heauen is quite forgot.

(x, 22–28)

This verse hardly suggests Shakespeare. Several prose
passages are far superior, but one may well doubt whether a
suspicion of Shakespeare's participation would ever have
arisen had the evidence for it been restricted to that within
the play itself. Of all the plays in the Shakespeare apocrypha, however, it is for *A Yorkshire Tragedy* that there is
the strongest external evidence for Shakespeare's authorship. Not only was it printed in 1608 with the declaration
on the title-page that it had been "Written by W. Shakspeare" and "Acted by his maiesties Players at the Globe,"
but it was in the same year entered as a work by "Wylliam
Shakespere" upon the Register of the Stationers' Company.[35]

Yet this apparently strong external evidence for Shakespeare's authorship is, I think, to a great extent weakened
by other external evidence which may argue against his
authorship. Much of this has been made available only recently—too late for it to be fully appreciated by earlier
critics, many of whom, contrary to their inclinations and
critical judgments, bowed before what they thought the
overwhelming external evidence and sought to find some-
where in the play passages which Shakespeare might have
written. The comparatively recent unraveling of the
mystery of the 1619 quartos has shown Thomas Pavier,
the publisher of *A Yorkshire Tragedy* and the one to whom
it was entered on the Register, to have been an utterly
unscrupulous publisher, ready for financial gain not only to
make false ascriptions but to forge dates and even whole

title-pages.[36] The honesty of any enterprise in which Pavier was a principal is, therefore, suspect. As he and Nathaniel Butter were birds of a like feather, the title-page of *A Yorkshire Tragedy*, were it not for the entry in the Register, would carry no more credence than that of *The London Prodigal*. And we may well be suspicious of this entry not alone because it was made to Pavier but as well because of the rarity of the entries which cite the authors of dramatic pieces.[37] On only two occasions was Shakespeare's name cited when plays by him were entered. The second date was 27 November 1607 when *King Lear* was entered, and here the fullness of detail must have been deemed necessary to distinguish Shakespeare's play from the older *Leir*, which had been entered to others in 1605.[38] The other date is 23 August 1600, when *Much Ado* and *2 Henry IV* were entered as by "W. Shakespeare." An explanation of this ascription is not hard to find. Less than three weeks before (4 August) a note had been made on the Register that the printing of *Much Ado* (and *As You Like It, Every Man in his Humour*, and *Henry V*) was "to be staid." [39] The inclusion of Shakespeare's name in the entries of 23 August may therefore have been intended to identify the plays more definitely and to indicate that permission for their printing had been obtained.

And finally there is, of course, strong argument against Shakespeare's authorship in the omission of *A Yorkshire Tragedy* from the First Folio of 1623. John Heminge and Henry Condell, who were later to bring together the dramatic works of their friend and fellow, are both known to have been members of Shakespeare's company for a number of years prior to the Calverley murders—for nine and seven years respectively. Had Shakespeare written a drama-

tized account of these murders, they would most certainly
have known of it, possibly have acted in it, and presumably
have included it in their collection of 1623, for the title-
page claims that *A Yorkshire Tragedy* had been acted by
the company in which they were both actors and shareholders. That Heminge and Condell, who claim that they
are including "all" the plays written by Shakespeare, should
have discarded one which had been previously credited to
him and the text of which must have been readily available
—in printed form if not among the company's playbooks—
must be recognized as very strong evidence against Shakespeare's authorship.

The omission of *A Yorkshire Tragedy* from the First
Folio, the obviously unscrupulous dealings of Thomas
Pavier, and the suspicions occasioned by the inexplicable
entry of the author's name in the Stationers' Register, although they must be regarded as grounds for doubting
Shakespeare's authorship of the play, cannot, of course, be
said to indicate that Shakespeare may not, when the play
was being prepared for the stage, have introduced here and
there lines which he thought might render the play more
effective. That he may have done for any play presented
by his company. If, however, Pavier be convicted of bad
faith, there would appear to be no more reason to suspect
insertions by Shakespeare in *A Yorkshire Tragedy* than in
any other plays known to have been acted by his company.
Nonetheless a number of critics, though convinced that
Shakespeare's part in the play was very small indeed, have
persuaded themselves that the external evidence justifies
the belief that he must have had at least some connection
with it. Few since Steevens [40] have been ready to accept
Shakespeare's sole authorship and none has agreed with A.

W. Schlegel's confident assertion that *A Yorkshire Tragedy*
(and *Cromwell* and *Sir John Oldcastle* as well) was "not
only unquestionably Shakespeare's but deserved to be
classed among his best and maturest works." [41]

The struggle occasioned by the conflict between the internal evidence of the play itself and what they thought
the strong external evidence is reflected in the discussions
of Collier, Ulrici, Fleay, and others. Collier expressed the
belief that Shakespeare must have been "concerned" in the
play, but the weight he gave to the external evidence is
to be seen in his claim that "the internal evidence . . . of
Shakespeare's authorship is nearly as strong as the external,
and there are some speeches which could scarcely have proceeded from any other pen." Recognizing, however, that
such "has not been the general opinion of commentators"
and that the matter of the tragedy is unlike that one might
expect him to choose, he suggested that "perhaps [Shake-
speare] yielded to the necessity of the case and . . . contributed this one of four short plays presented the same
night." [42]

Ulrici, whose discussion, though largely drawn from
Collier's, is stated with greater boldness, expressed the conviction that "Every unprejudiced reader of the 'Yorkshire
Tragedy' will . . . recognize the hand of Shakespeare,
not only in the composition, in spite of its great simplicity,
but also in the characters and the language"; some passages "can have proceeded from no other pen than
Shakespeare's." Yet apparently not wholly satisfied, he
suggested that Shakespeare may have undertaken the play
"at the request of his brother actors, who wished to gratify
the momentary excitement of the public," and have had
"neither time to give it perfection at the first nor inclination

afterwards to alter and improve it." [43] Its omission from
the Folio might be explained, he further suggested, by
the play's having been quite forgotten after the popular
interest in the murders had subsided. This second suggestion is rendered quite unacceptable by Pavier's having published a second quarto of *A Yorkshire Tragedy*, again ascribed to Shakespeare, as one of the ten plays brought
out in his venture of 1619. There is no doubt the King's
Men knew of this venture, for they took steps to check it.
It would appear certain, therefore, that when Heminge
and Condell brought out the First Folio four years later,
they knew *A Yorkshire Tragedy* had been ascribed to
Shakespeare and, had they wished to include it, could easily
have secured the text.

A Yorkshire Tragedy caused F. G. Fleay no little agony
and led him to propound two of his most extraordinary
theories. Reluctantly yielding to what he thought strong
external evidence,[44] he first suggested that the tragedy
may have been written by Edmund Shakespeare, player,
buried at St. Saviour's, Southwark, 31 December 1607,
age 27. "Of Edmund's career in London," continued Fleay,
"we *know* nothing; but surely he must have belonged to
the Globe company. His absence from the actors' lists
offers no obstacle to this suggestion; they are, after that
of *The Seven Deadly Sins* in 1594, confined to names of
shareholders and principal actors. And if player for the
Globe, why not author? May he not, for instance, have
written *The Yorkshire Tragedy* under his brother's super-
intendence, and may not this account for its being published
as William Shakespeare's?" [45] Later, however, declaring
that "The external evidence of authorship is exactly the
same for *The Yorkshire Tragedy* as for *Pericles*," Fleay

suggested that *A Yorkshire Tragedy* may have been the original ending of an earlier version of *The Miseries of Enforced Marriage*, an ending which Wilkins discarded upon deciding to give that play a happy ending.[46] How untenable I think this second theory, I have already tried to show.

Swinburne, too, wavered. Although he first stated his conviction that the *Tragedy* could not have been written by Shakespeare, he later came around to the view that Shakespeare's authorship was at least not incredible.[47] Sir A. W. Ward, and perhaps most who today may be inclined to see Shakespeare's hand in the play at all, would assign him no more than an "incidental share"—the prose speech of Husband in scene iv beginning "O thou confused man" and the "subsequent affecting scene" between Husband and his young son.[48] One may well ask, however, whether these few speeches, good though they be, would ever have been thought to be by Shakespeare had his name not appeared on the title-page.

The extent to which it has been felt that the 1608 ascription must have at least some justification, even though the *Tragedy* be recognized as not "Written by W. Shakspeare," is illustrated by a recent article by Mr. Marc Friedlaender, who ingeniously but most strangely argued that the entry of the play upon the Stationers' Register as by Shakespeare proved that Pavier thought it by him, and that the play must, therefore, have been sold him as Shakespeare's work, which would command a higher price than would work by other dramatists. "If then Shakespeare had nothing to do with *A Yorkshire Tragedy*," he wrote, "we must assume acquiescence in the deception both by Shakespeare and by the dramatist who actually wrote the play, and duplicity on

the part of the managers of the company. . . . there is
no reason to believe that the Burbages or their associates
would have resorted to such methods in order to turn a
profit." [49] Accordingly Friedlaender suggested, as has been
earlier noted, that Shakespeare wrote scene i to render the
play less liable to restraint by the authorities. Hence the
"Written by W. Shakspeare." Such an explanation obviously does not go far toward absolving the participants
of deception and duplicity. If after he had added only a
short opening scene to a play by another, the Burbages
or their associates had sold the play to Pavier as Shakespeare's, they were still guilty of gross duplicity and Shakespeare no less to be blamed for acquiescence in the deception. Shakespeare, indeed, unless he took steps to correct
the error, was guilty of something worse. No blame can
be attached to him if without his knowledge a play by another was published as by him, but it would be quite different if he took another's play, added a brief scene, and
then without offering a protest, saw the whole play first
sold and then printed as by him.

Most of the critics, Pope,[50] Malone,[51] William Hazlitt,[52] Halliwell-Phillipps,[53] Tyrrell,[54] Knight,[55] Moorman,[56] Lee,[57] Tucker Brooke,[58] and Sir Edmund Chambers [59] among others, have with varying certainty of
conviction denied Shakespeare's participation in any way
whatsoever. To them the evidence within the play seemed
sufficient to outweigh what external evidence for his authorship they recognized. Because of Thomas Heywood's inclination toward domestic tragedy and the excellence of
his *A Woman Killed with Kindness*, it is not surprising
that Heywood was early suggested as the real author of
A Yorkshire Tragedy; but beyond such assertions as that

the play is "decidedly in the manner of Heywood," [60] a case for his authorship was not made until 1931, when Mr. A. M. Clark published his *Thomas Heywood, Playwright and Miscellanist*. The case there presented for Heywood could only have disappointed those who had been inclined to favor his authorship. After noting that Heywood was a master of the genre of domestic tragedy, Mr. Clark devoted the next four pages to arguing that Shakespeare was not the author. Then, though he had obviously read *Two Unnatural Murthers*, he proceeded to argue that "The Master of a College, the various country gentlemen, the Knight and the maid are the usual supernumeraries of Heywood's plays." [61] All of them are, of course, lifted intact from the tract. "Their [Husband's and Wife's] striking resemblance to young Arthur and his wife in *How a Man may Choose a Good Wife* is itself almost proof of Heywood's authorship. The husband's character is made up of the same ingredients as young Arthur's, coarseness, pride, selfishness, and brutality. . . . The Wife is another of Heywood's loving, submissive women. . . . Like Mrs. Arthur she bears all her husband's insults with quiet dignity." [62] And finally, "the reconciliation in the last scene of the *Tragedy* has no parallel except in Heywood's own theatre." The reconciliation has, of course, a parallel in the tract; it as well as the characters and the behavior of Husband and Wife is presented in the play in exactly the same way, often in the same words, as in *Two Unnatural Murthers*. If only Heywood were capable of presenting such scenes and such characters, Heywood must also have written the *Two Unnatural Murthers* and, presumably, have there departed from the actual facts of the case in order to introduce his favorite situations and characters. That Mr.

Clark does not suggest. He cites certain parallels in thought, not in language, between the *Tragedy* and *How a Man may Choose* and *Philocothonista*, and then notes that Chapter V of Heywood's *Curtain Lecture* (1637) is on *The Miseries of enforced contracts*, and that there is an actual allusion to the Calverley murders in *Philocothonista* (1635). In *A Yorkshire Tragedy*, as repeatedly noted, there is not the faintest suggestion of an enforced marriage, and the passage in *Philocothonista* (1635), far from suggesting that Heywood had himself written a play on the Calverley murders, urges rather that he would have regarded a stage presentation of the story as in bad taste:

One Master Coverlee, a gentleman of quality and good dissent, in the like distemper wounded his Wife and slew his own Children; whom I am bolder to nominate, because the facinerous act hath by authority bin licensed to be acted on the publicke stage.[63]

In 1906 Bertram Dobell advanced the claim of another dramatist.[64] Whether or not he was in part influenced by the 1608 ascriptions of *A Yorkshire Tragedy* to Shakespeare, Dobell recognized his hand in both that play and *Miseries of Enforced Marriage*. In both he thought "there are so many passages which seem to bear the stamp of [Shakespeare's] style that I can hardly doubt that they received the benefit of his revision, and were most likely fitted for the stage by him." [65] The non-Shakespearean and the greater parts of both plays he assigned of course to George Wilkins, who he thought had contributed to *Timon, Pericles,* and *Macbeth*. Promising to present further evidence at a later time, Dobell in this note supported Wilkins' authorship of *A Yorkshire Tragedy* by stating that both plays have the same "intensity" and seem to have been written by a "coarse-minded and coarse-natured man"; both have many riming lines, many broken lines, and many "prose passages the style of which is evidently imitated from Shakespeare's style"; and in both there is frequent repetition of words and phrases. Such repetition is found in many dramatists, as are rimed couplets and broken lines; and one may ask whether the impression of a coarse-nature and coarse-mindedness comes not rather from the plot than from the nature and mind of the poet.

Although Dobell died eight years later without fulfilling his promise to make a fuller case for Wilkins' authorship, Mr. H. Dugdale Sykes in 1917 vigorously presented an almost identical view.[66] He recognized at times in *A Yorkshire Tragedy* a superior hand, but the real author of both plays he argued was George Wilkins. Although the *Miseries* is the only extant play ascribed wholly to Wilkins, Mr. Sykes brought together from it, from Acts I and II of *Pericles* and scattered bits of other works possibly by Wilkins, a number of verbal parallels to *A Yorkshire Tragedy* which, like any array of parallels, seems momentarily impressive. Yet he himself observed that "If the evidence of the parallel passages stood alone, it would scarcely justify us in attributing the *Tragedy* to Wilkins." He insisted, however, that the evidence of parallel passages "is confirmed not only by the metrical characteristics of the play but by its peculiarities of grammar and vocabulary." [67] The word "peculiarities" is hardly justified, for Mr. Sykes made no effort to establish the fact that what he regarded as "peculiarities" of Wilkins are indeed peculiar to him and not found in the work of any or all of his contemporaries. He was impressed by several instances of omission of the relative pronoun—"a confirmed habit of Wilkins," he declared. But, one may ask, of how many others? Abbott,[68] for example, notes that such omissions are frequent in Shakespeare, and one can but suspect them common in the verse of many.

Similarly unimpressive is Mr. Sykes' observation that Wilkins shows "a curious partiality for lines ending in polysyllabic words in -tion. There are five such in the *Tragedy*. Where they are of regular decasyllabic metre it is to be noticed that the *-tion* is clearly pronounced as a dissyllable." [69] There is no peculiarity here. Again to quote Abbott on Shakespeare's usage: "The termination 'ion' is frequently pronounced as two syllables at the end of a line" though "cases in which *ion* is pronounced in the middle of a line are rare." [70] Nor, I suspect, is the use of the prefatory "Why" in any way peculiar to Wilkins. Mr. Sykes wrote of its "constant recurrence" in *A Yorkshire Tragedy;* but except in scene i, where there are six instances of it, it appears only four times in the play. Today, surely, the prefatory "Why" is widely used in conversation; doubtless it was also used in Jacobean days. Middleton often introduced it, and so I should suspect, until evidence to the contrary is presented, did many who sought to reproduce conversational speech.

Equally unimpressive are, I believe, the other "peculiarities" noted by Mr. Sykes: the "frequent idiomatic use of the word 'tricks' " (twice in the *Miseries* and three times in the *Tragedy*), the appearance in both plays of "dust" with the meaning of "money" and of rimed couplets in which "this voice" is used in the sense of opinion. Even though it were shown, as it cannot yet be, that some of these uses are indeed peculiar to George Wilkins, may not the similarities between *A Yorkshire Tragedy* and *The*

Miseries be sufficiently explained by Wilkins' having made use of the earlier play. That he did make use of it is clear enough, even though it appears he must have known another account as well.

Nothing that I have written, of course, argues against Wilkins having written *A Yorkshire Tragedy*. He may well have acquired additional information later, and the minor differences within the two plays (such as the period during which the husband and wife lived together, the number of their children, the responsibility of the guardian) may be explained, like the happy ending, to his altered purpose in the later play. Nothing could be more reasonable than that the author of *A Yorkshire Tragedy*, when the attraction of that occasional piece was thought diminishing, should have set himself to rework it into a fresh and complete five-act play. The only argument that can now be made against Wilkins' authorship—other, of course, than by demonstrating another's authorship—is that there are in the *Tragedy* a much greater dramatic power and at times a deeper insight into the human soul than are to be discovered in the one play which can be confidently ascribed to Wilkins. Such an argument may be quite unfair to him. We have no known tragedy from his pen, and certainly much of the power and effectiveness of *A Yorkshire Tragedy* would inevitably disappear if, to lengthen it into a five-act play, "the breathless heat" of its action were sacrificed by the alternating of the scenes which depict the sufferings of Husband and Wife with those presenting such subplots as the stories of Scarborow's sister and brothers.

All that can or should, I believe, be said at present of the authorship of the *Tragedy* is this. If it be denied, as practically all critics have denied, that shortly after writing *Lear* and *Macbeth* William Shakespeare could have been the sole or even the principal author of *A Yorkshire Tragedy*, we may be justified in concluding that the 1608 ascriptions to him were due to either an innocent error or a deliberate fraud—and Pavier's unsavory reputation strongly suggests the latter. Whether innocent or fraudulent, however, the ascription is thoroughly unambiguous and must, therefore, be accepted or rejected in entirety. If rejected, it must be recognized that it provides no external evidence for Shakespeare's participation in the tragedy in any way. Although it is possible, of course, if the play were acted by his company, that Shakespeare may have revised or appended a speech or two here and there, as he may have done in many another play presented by his company, the 1608 ascription of the play to him can hardly be said to offer the slightest external evidence of his having done so. A convincing identification of the author or authors of *A Yorkshire Tragedy*, if it is ever to be accomplished, must await our clearer knowledge of what were the peculiar characteristics of the various Jacobean dramatists.

NOTES

1. Walter W. Greg, ed., *Henslowe's Diary* (2 vols., London, A. H. Bullen, 1904), I, 113. There is little doubt that the correct date of the quarto bearing Shakespeare's name is 1619, though the title-page carries the forged date 1600. See E. K. Chambers, *William Shakespeare* (2 vols., Oxford, Clarendon Press, 1930), I, 133ff. The anonymous first quarto appeared in 1599. The authors were Munday, Drayton, Wilson, and Hathway.

2.   (1) *Looking Glass for London* (Ent. S.R. to Creede, 5 March 1594)

     (2) *True Tragedy of Richard III* (Ent. to Creede, 19 June 1594)

     (3) *Selimus* (No entry)

     (4) *The Pedlar's Prophecy* (Ent. to Creede, 13 May 1594)

     (5) *Menaechmi* (Ent. to Creede, 10 June 1594)

     (6) *Locrine* (Ent. to Creede, 20 July 1594)

     (7) *The Famous Victories of Henry V* (Ent. to Creede, 14 May 1594)

     (8) *James IV* (Ent. to Creede, 14 May 1594)

     (9) *Alphonsus King of Aragon* (No entry)

     (10) *Clyomon and Clamydes* (No entry)

3. When *Cornelia* was printed in 1594, the title-page offered no indication of its author, but that the publishers were aware of its authorship is shown by the entry in the Stationers' Register,

26 January 1594, to N. Linge and J. Busby of "CORNELIA, Thomas Kydd beinge the authour." See Edward Arber, *A Transcript of the Registers of the Company of Stationers of London* (5 vols., London, privately printed, 1875–77), II, 644.

4. (1) *The Three Lords of London,* 1590, "by R.W. . . . Printed by R. Ihones."

(2) *Tancred and Gismund,* 1591, "Newly reuiued and polished according to the decorum of these daies. *By R.W. Printed by Thomas Scarlet . . . to be solde by* R. Robinson."

(3) *Menaechmi,* 1595, "Written in English by *W. W.* . . . Printed by Tho. Creede . . . to be sold by William Barley."

(4) *Locrine,* 1595, "Newly set foorth, ouerseene and corrected, By *W.S.* . . . Printed by Thomas Creede."

(5) *The Old Wives Tale,* 1595, "Written by *G.P.* Printed . . . by *Iohn Danter . . .* to be sold by *Raph Hancocke,* and *Iohn Hardie.*"

(6) *Alphonsus King of Aragon,* 1599. "Made by *R.G.* . . . Printed by Thomas Creede."

(7) *An Humorous Day's Mirth,* 1599. "*By G. C. . . . Printed by Valentine Syms.*"

(8) *Every Man out of his Humour,* 1600. "*As it was first composed by the* AUTHOR B.I. *Containing more than hath been Publickely Spoken or Acted* . . . Printed for *William Holme.*"

(9) *Antonio and Mellida,* 1602. "Written by *I.M. . . .* Printed for *Mathewe Lownes,* and *Thomas Fisher.*"

(10) *Antonio's Revenge,* 1602. "Written by *I.M. . . .* Printed for *Thomas Fisher.*"

(11) *Thomas Lord Cromwell*, 1602, "Written by W.S. Imprinted . . . for *William Iones*."

(12) *The Puritan*, 1607. "Written by W.S. Imprinted . . . by G. Eld."

(13) *A Mad World My Masters*, 1608. "Composed by T.M. . . . Printed by *H.B.* for Walter Bvrre."

(14) *A Trick to Catch the Old One*, having first been printed by George Eld in 1608, without indication of authorship, was within the same year reissued with "Composde by T.M. . . . Printed by *G: E.* . . . to be sold by *Henry Rockytt*."

5. The two parts of *The Contention* had properly been published as anonymous and can hardly be regarded, in the texts they present, as plays by Shakespeare.

6. Though entered on the Stationers' Register 7 September 1580, the earliest extant edition is that of 1597.

7. Arber, *Transcript*, III, 153.

8. *The Library*, 3d Ser., II (1911), 231.

9. E. K. Chambers, *The Elizabethan Stage* (4 vols., Clarendon Press, 1923), II, 127; III, 495.

10. *Henslowe's Diary*, I, 6; II, 312.

11. Chambers, *Elizabethan Stage*, II, 339.

12. In addition to Wentworth Smith and the author of *Hector of Germany*, whom I discuss, there is, as Sir Edmund Chambers notes, "A 'Smith,' whose *Fair Foul One* Herbert licensed on 28 Nov. 1623," and "if Warburton can be trusted, a 'Will Smithe,' whose *St. George for England* his cook burnt" (*Elizabethan Stage*, III, 493).

13. Chambers, *Elizabethan Stage*, III, 493.

14. This play, edited as a University of Pennsylvania doctoral thesis by L. W. Payne, was published in 1906.

15. Heywood's comments in the epistle to *The Rape of Lu-*

crece and in the prologue for a revival of *If You Know not Me.*

16. Chambers, *Elizabethan Stage,* III, 191.

17. Chambers, *William Shakespeare,* I, 536.

18. For a discussion and bibliography of the fraudulent publications of 1619, see Chambers, *William Shakespeare,* I, 135–36.

19. The play was entered to William Cotton on 11 August 1602, and no record survives of a transfer to Jones. There is little doubt, however, that Jones acquired the rights, for on 16 December 1611 he transferred to John Browne the "booke called the lyfe and death of the Lord Cromwell, by W: S." (Arber, *Transcript,* III, 214, 474).

20. *Henslowe's Diary,* II, 208.

21. Arber, *Transcript,* II, 839.

22. Arber, *Transcript,* III, 37.

23. Chambers, *Elizabethan Stage,* III, 191.

24. Arber, *Transcript,* II, 823. Nonetheless John Wilkinson was seven years later, 19 April 1602, admitted freeman of the Company.

I: The Lamentable Tragedy of Locrine

1. Edward Arber, *A Transcript of the Register of the Company of Stationers of London* (5 vols., London, privately printed, 1875), II, 656.

2. An allusion to the queen in the closing speech of the play, indeed, suggests that the quarto did not appear before late 1595 or 1596:

> So let vs pray for that renowned mayd,
>
> That eight and thirtie yeares the scepter swayd,
>
> In quiet peace and sweet felicitie. (lines 2276–78)

3. Such seems to have been Fleay's idea when he wrote: "I

have faith in the view that W. S., who saw this play through the press between 1595 Nov. and 1596 Mar., was W. Shakespeare, and that he did it from charity to his old coadjutor [Peele], 'long sick and in necessity,' 17th Jan. 1596, when he sent his *Tale of Troy* to L. Burleigh . . ." See Frederick G. Fleay, *Biographical Chronicle of the English Drama* (2 vols., London, Reeves, 1891), II, 321.

4. Preface to the Malone Society reprint (Oxford, H. Hart, 1908), p. v.

5. Compare F. S. Moorman, *Cambridge History of English Literature*, Vol. V (1910), Ch. X: "The words 'newlie set foorth, ouerseene and corrected' indicate that *Locrine* was an old play revised in 1591."

6. Theodor Erbe, *Die Locrinesage und die Quellen des pseudo-Shakespeareschen Locrine* (Vol. XVI of *Studien zur englischen Philologie*, Halle, 1904).

7. Willard Farnham, "John Higgins' *Mirror* and *Locrine*," *Modern Philology*, XXIII (1925–26), 307–13.

8. The Malone Society reprint (1908) is the edition of *Locrine* to which references are made and from which lines are quoted. Quotations from *The Mirror for Magistrates* are from the text edited by Miss Lily B. Campbell (Cambridge, The University Press, 1946); those from Geoffrey of Monmouth's *History* from the translation in the Everyman Library.

As the more usual form of the title is *A Mirror for Magistrates*, I hope I may not be charged with pedantry if, to escape a suspicion of slovenliness, I note that although the early editions (1559, 1563, 1571) bear the title *A Mirror for Magistrates*, the stories of Locrine and Albanact first appear in the supplementary volume of 1574, *The first part of the Mirror for Magistrates*. This first part was in 1587 reissued with the second part of 1578 under the title *The Mirror for Magistrates*,

and it was probably this text which was used by the author of
Locrine. Well after the publication of *Locrine* the original title,
A Mirror for Magistrates, was resumed in the complete edition
of 1610.

9. Reprinted in Vol. II of *The Complete Works of Thomas
Lodge*. Printed for the Hunterian Club, 1883. Quotations are
from this reprint.

10. The supposed reference, which is in the epilogue (lines
2271–72), if to Queen Mary, need not have been made before
her execution.

11. See "Plagiate im *Locrine*" by Rudolf Brotanek in *Bei-
blatt zur Anglia*, XI (1900), 202–7; and "Edmund Spenser,
'Locrine,' and 'Selimus'" by Charles Crawford in *Notes and
Queries*, 9th Ser., VII (1901), 61 *et al*. The Address to the
Reader prefixed to the 1591 volume leaves no doubt that for
some time prior to their publication Spenser's poems "were dis-
perst abroad in sundrie hands." It is therefore possible, though
unsafe to assume, that the author of *Locrine* knew the poems in
manuscript.

12. See "'Locrine' and the 'Faerie Queene'" by Carrie A.
Harper in *Modern Language Review*, VII (1913), 369–71.

13. In the older accounts Estrild is sometimes called Humber's daughter, but more often the daughter of a German king,
abducted by Humber on an earlier raid. Erbe notes that it is
only in this play that she is called Humber's wife, "though she
is by her enemies labelled Humber's concubine" (p. 68). Except in this scene, where both Locrine and Estrild herself imply
her married state (though she calls herself "the Scithians paramour" later in the scene, line 1534), only Guendoline and
Ate, the speaker of the choruses, mention her position. To them
she is a concubine (cf. lines 1371, 1785, 1917, 2166).

14. It may be noted that these lines are somewhat reminis-

cent of a demand made by King Rasni in Greene's and Lodge's *Looking Glass for London and England* (printed 1594):

How now, what meane these outcries in our Court?

(line 1153).

15. Crawford, "Edmund Spenser, 'Locrine' and 'Selimus,' " *Notes and Queries*, 9th Ser., VII (1901), 61, 101, 142, 203, 261, 324, 384.

16. E. Koeppel, " 'Locrine' und 'Selimus' " in *Jahrbuch der deutschen Shakespeare-Gesellschaft*, XLI (1905), 193–99.

17. Frank G. Hubbard, *"Locrine* and *Selimus"* in *Shakespeare Studies* by Members of the Department of English in the University of Wisconsin (Madison, 1916), pp. 17–35.

18. Hubbard, *"Locrine* and *Selimus,"* p. 25.

19. Hubbard, *"Locrine* and *Selimus,"* p. 27.

20. Hubbard, *"Locrine* and *Selimus,"* p. 22.

21. Richard Knolles, *The Generall Historie of the Turkes* (3d ed., 1621), pp. 495, 501–2.

22. Cf. *Two very notable commentaries* . . . by Andre Cambine, translated by John Shute (London, 1562): Corcut "determyned to se yf he moughte by flighte saue his lyfe . . . & when he came to the passage he founde it, with all the sea coaste occupied with the galleys . . . of Selim, and whē he sawe no meanes howe to gette oute of the countre, he determyned to hide him in certaine woodes there at hand, and when he contynued there in caues for a certaine tyme and lyued of wylde hony, and rootes . . ." (foll. 54v–55); and *A shorte treatise vpon the Turkes Chronicles,* compiled by Paulus Jovius . . . and translated out of Latyne into englysh by Peter Ashton (London, 1546): Corcuthus, learning of Selimus' plan to kill him, "changed his apparel, and fled . . . to the sea banke of Smyrna, & there skulking in a certayne denne, loked for some shyppe, whiche shoulde passe that waye to Rhodes. But after

he perceyued that . . . his expectation was al in vayne, he yssued (compelled by hunger) oute of his caue, and soone after (by faleshead of his seruant) he was betrayed, and taken, . . ." (foll. lxix).

23. J. Churton Collins, *The Plays and Poems of Robert Greene* (2 vols., Oxford, Clarendon Press, 1905), I, 64–67.

24. Quoted in *Shakespeare's Dramatic Art* . . . translated from the German of Dr. Hermann Ulrici (London, Chapman Brothers, 1846), p. 441.

25. August Wilhelm Schlegel, *A Course of Lectures on Dramatic Art and Literature*, translated by John Black (London, Bell, 1846), p. 444. The question of Shakespeare's authorship he thought "immediately connected with that respecting *Titus Andronicus*, and must with it be resolved in the affirmative or negative."

26. Ulrici, *Shakespeare's Dramatic Art*, p. 443. A. F. Hopkinson saw the play as Peele's revised by Shakespeare; see *Locrine* (ed. 1892), pp. ixff. and "An Essay on Locrine" in *Essays on Shakespeare's Doubtful Plays* (London, 1900), pp. xiiiff.

27. R. Simpson in a review of Wolfgang Bernhardi's *Robert Greene's Leben und Schriften* (*The Academy*, 21 March 1874, p. 310) wrote: "I imagine that W. S., the 'ironical censurer' of other men, who had been accused of stealing from Marlowe and Greene and Peele, was willing to show what manner of plays his would be if he imitated those models; and therefore that he interpolated passages from Greene and Peele into the stilted and tedious old tragedy of *Locrine*, and so set it forth 'ouerseen and corrected by W. S.' "

Equally remarkable, and not wholly dissimilar, was the view expressed by Arthur Acheson in *Shakespeare, Chapman and Sir Thomas More* (New York, Hackett, 1931). According to

Acheson, *Locrine* was originally penned by Greene in 1585–86
and later corrected by Shakespeare, though "the only correc-
tion made by Shakespeare . . . was in the fourth line from the
end, where the words 'eight and thirty years,' which coincide
with the date of publication in 1595, took the place of a number
indicating either its date of composition or of its previous presentation." Acheson argued that Creede's statement that the
play had been "Newly set foorth, ouerseene and corrected, By
W. S." was not only authorized but actually dictated by William Shakespeare, who undertook the "mildly ironical gesture"
of so printing the play in order to show his unconcern at the
"personal caricature" of him in the part of Strumbo "as a lover
and a writer of ardent and fiery love epistles" (pp. 160–61).
Strumbo, it must be admitted, does in his first appearance pen
a love epistle, but it is difficult to imagine how he could have
been identified with Shakespeare or why Shakespeare should
have waited so long—until three years after his attacker's death
—before thus demonstrating his unconcern. Indeed, such a delayed answer would rather indicate that a deep hurt had been
long harbored in silence.

    28. Edmund Malone, *Supplement to Shakespeare* (1780),
II, 187–264. Quoted by Bakeless, *The Tragicall History of
Christopher Marlowe* (2 vols., Harvard University Press,
1942), II, 281–82.

    29. Samuel Hickson, "Marlowe and the Old 'Taming of
a Shrew,'" *Notes and Queries*, 1st Ser., I (1850), 194.

    30. *Cambridge History of English Literature*, V, 267.

    31. He first assigned the play to Peele, then to Charles
Tilney with revisions by Peele, and finally again to Peele. The
ascription to Charles Tilney rested upon a much disputed note
to which J. P. Collier called attention (*Catalogue Bibliographi-
cal and Critical*, 1837, p. 41)—a note signed G. B., "believed

from the handwriting to be the initials of Sir George Buck."
The note, which has been slightly cut at the edge, has been
expanded by Sir Walter Greg to read:

> Char. Tilney wrot$<$e a$>$
> Tragedy of this mattr$<$wch$>$
> hee named Estrild: $<$& wch$>$
> I think is this. it was $<$lost ?$>$
> by his death. & now (?) $<$some$>$
> fellow hath published $<$it$>$
> I made dūbe shewes for it.
> Wch I yet have. G. B.

The genuineness of this note, which in 1930 was in the posses-
sion of A. S. W. Rosenbach, has been attacked by Dr. S. A.
Tannenbaum in *Shaksperian Scraps* (New York, Columbia
University Press, 1933), pp. 36–41, and defended by Sir
Walter Greg in "Three Manuscript Notes by Sir George Buc"
in *The Library*, 4th Ser., XII (1931), 307–21, and Professor
R. C. Bald in "The *Locrine* and *George-a-Greene* Title-page
Inscriptions" in *The Library*, 4th Ser., XV (1934), 295–305.
There is, of course, no other evidence that Tilney wrote any
dramatic pieces. As a conspirator he was hanged and quartered
for high treason on 20 Sept. 1586. Whether or not the note is
genuine, whether or not Tilney wrote a play named "Estrild,"
little of a play by him can be preserved in *Locrine*, although it
would be amusingly ironical that a play by the convicted conspirator should when published have, as *Locrine* has in great
abundance, lines such as

> So perish that they [i.e. they that] enuie Brittaines wealth,
> So let them die with endlesse infamie;
> And he that seekes his soueraignes ouerthrow,
> Would this my club might aggrauate his woe;

(lines 1290–93)

and with an epilogue which, after asking prayers for Elizabeth, closes with:

And euery wight that seekes her graces smart,
wold that this sword wer pierced in his hart.

Certainly the dumb shows which appear in *Locrine* were not contrived by Buck for Tilney's play. Two of them—most clearly that preceding Act III—must have been suggested not alone by the succeeding events of the play but to a very large extent by Spenser's *Visions of the World's Vanity*, from which no fewer than nine lines are lifted for Ate's description of the dumb show of Act III.

32. Sir Adolphus W. Ward, *History of English Dramatic Literature* (3 vols., London and New York, Macmillan, 1899), II, 220.

33. W. S. Gaud, "The Authorship of *Locrine*" in *Modern Philology*, I (1904), 409–22.

34. Felix E. Schelling, *Elizabethan Drama, 1558–1642* (Boston and New York, Houghton Mifflin, 1908), I, 256.

35. Schelling, *Elizabethan Drama*, II, 404–5.

36. J. A. Symonds, *Shakespere's Predecessors* (London, Smith, Elder, 1884), p. 369.

37. C. F. Tucker Brooke, *The Shakespeare Apocrypha* (Oxford, Clarendon Press, 1908), p. xviii.

38. Brooke, *Shakespeare Apocrypha*, p. xix.

39. Brooke, *Shakespeare Apocrypha*, pp. 84–100.

40. It was long generally assumed that Lodge sailed with Cavendish 26 August 1591 and did not return until 11 June 1593. Professor C. J. Sisson has, however, shown that Lodge was back in England at least as early as February 1593 and cites reason to think he may have returned about May 1592; see *Thomas Lodge and other Elizabethans* (Cambridge, Mass., 1933), pp. 89, 105–6.

41. If the evidence presented be thought sufficient to urge
that *Locrine* was revised by the author of *Selimus*, there is perhaps another possible clue to its authorship which should be considered, however unlikely may seem the identification it suggests. Among the manuscripts of the Marquis of Bath at Longleat is a poem of fifty-nine lines headed "1603 Certaine hellish
verses devysed by that atheist and traitor Ralegh as it is said."
(Historical MSS Commission, *MSS of the Marquis of Bath*,
II, 52–53. The lines are reprinted by Jean Jacquot, "Ralegh's
'Hellish Verses' and the 'Tragicall Raigne of Selimus' " in *Modern Language Review*, XLVIII [1953], 1–9.) The verses
were certainly not written by Raleigh in 1603; save for a number of variants and the omission of four lines, the verses, as
M. Jacquot has pointed out, are identical to a passage in
Selimus (lines 305–67) in which that bloody usurper expresses
his contempt for religion as something created by man to force
obedience from lesser men. Below the last line of the poem in
the manuscript there appears "Finis R. W. alias W. Rawley."
A second MS copy of these verses, practically identical to the
copy at Longleat, is preserved in the British Museum, Add. MS
32092, f. 201. M. Jacquot declares "The title ['Certaine
hellish verses,' etc.] is the same as in the Longleat copy. So is
the end 'finis R. W. alias W. Rawley' " (p. 2 note).

Though M. Jacquot considered the possibility that the dramatist had obtained an unpublished poem by Raleigh and inserted
it into his play, he concluded, with reason, that the lines must
have been lifted from the play—presumably by an enemy who
sought to create prejudice against Raleigh in 1603. He noted,
however, that Selimus' arguments are not unlike views frequently
expressed by Raleigh and others of his circle and that the passage
is in part based upon authors known to Raleigh and used by him
in his *History of the World;* Raleigh's authorship, he thought,

"would not be entirely unthinkable if there existed any textual evidence in its favour and the verses had not, as they have, a dramatic significance which obliges us to consider them as belonging to the play."

M. Jacquot did not consider two other possible explanations: that *Selimus* itself may have been written by Raleigh—an explanation which none is likely to prefer, and that the one who attributed the lines to Raleigh did indeed cite the initials of the true author of the play, R. W., and stretched the truth only in identifying the initials as an alias of Sir Walter Raleigh.

The MS verses were clearly not copied directly from the only known edition of *Selimus*. Nor do the numerous variants seem wholly due to successive transcriptions, for the errors are hardly the sort which might be expected to result from a transcriber's inability to decipher what was before him. (Cf., for instance, *Selimus*, line 355: "Of actions tearmed by vs good or ill," with the MS: "as affections termeth us be it good or ill"; or line 359: "That Parricides, when death hath given them rest," with the MS: "that paradice when death doth give them rest.") Rather the "hellish verses" appear to represent an effort to reconstruct the passage in *Selimus* from memory or from hasty transcription in the theatre. Were a transcription made in the theatre, it need not, of course, have been made in 1603, and no such use need have been intended as that to which it was put by Raleigh's enemies. As M. Jacquot noted, the ideas set forth in Selimus' speech are strikingly similar to many attributed to and even spoken by members of Raleigh's group. It would seem not in the least strange that one of them, finding in the speech much to his liking, should about 1593 have arranged for a transcription to be made during performances of the play, and perhaps even presented a copy to Sir Walter. If the copy were later found among Raleigh's papers or among the papers of one known to have been an intimate, it would have been a natural inference that in "Finis R. W." the initials were merely the inverted initials of Walter Raleigh.

Yet it is surely possible that the initials were those of another. Perhaps they were the initials of the transcriber, who added "Finis R. W." to indicate that no additional portion of the speech had been transcribed. Again, since the initials R. W. fit Robert Wilson, who is known to have been writing for the stage shortly before *Selimus* appeared, one may query whether Wilson could have been the author of *Selimus* and the "Finis R. W." intended to credit the verses to him. Only three plays by Wilson are known to survive: *The Three Ladies of London* (printed 1584) and *The Three Lords and Ladies of London* (printed 1590), both on their title-pages declared to have been written by R. W., and *The Cobbler's Prophecy* (printed 1594), "Written by Robert Wilson, Gent." To the two earlier plays neither *Selimus* nor *Locrine* bears the slightest resemblance, nor perhaps is their faint resemblance to *The Cobbler's Prophecy* other than coincidental. While probably no plays of the period appropriated so extensively as did *Locrine* and *Selimus* the phraseology of other plays and poems, especially those by Greene, Peele, and Spenser, no comparable plagiarism or repetition has been detected in the plays by Wilson, although Miss Sisson has noted in *The Cobbler's Prophecy* "plagiarism of certain writings of Robert Greene: namely, *Never Too Late* (1590), . . . *Farewell to Folly* (1591), . . . and part three of the *Connie-Catching* pamphlets (1592)." See Sarah Trumbull Sisson, *The Coblers Prophesie: A Morality* edited with an Introduction and Notes. An abstract of a thesis. (Urbana, Illinois, 1942), 13 pp., p. 7. Only from *Farewell to Folly*, however, did she find "a complete 'lifting' of a line." Both *Locrine* and *Selimus*, as previously noted, appropriate a number of lines from Spenser's *Complaints* (1591); that Wilson may have known at least *Tears of the Muses* may be suggested by the somewhat forced entry of Clio, Melpomine, and Thalia into *The Prophecy,* where the muses complain not of the low esteem in which the poet is held but that the times afford no themes worthy their writing. Often in *The Prophecy* and in *Selimus,* but in only one scene of *Locrine,* the dialogue is framed in the six-line stanza riming *a b a b c c.* The closest resemblances, however, seem to be in the comic situations. Strumbo in *Locrine* and Raph in *The Prophecy* reappear repeatedly, both changing in character to fit into differing and largely unrelated situations. In II, iii, Strumbo enters with a stool and, while cobbling shoes, sings a song in praise of the cobbler's merry life; so in *The Prophecy* Raph Cobbler enters "with his stoole, his implements and shooes, and sitting on his stoole, falls to sing" (lines 52–53). It seems of little significance that both Raph and Strumbo have shrewish wives and that both are inducted into the army; in *The Prophecy* it is not Raph but the Countryman who is, like Strumbo, unwillingly pressed. Finally, and probably of even less significance, in *The Prophecy* the messenger Mercury, sent by the gods to bring about the events presented in the play, casts spells over Raph and his wife; in a comic scene in *Locrine* Humber mistakes the clownish Strumbo for Mercury, sent to relieve his hunger.

None of these similarities appears striking. Although I suspect that some of the blank verse of *The Prophecy* could, if imbedded in *Locrine,* pass unsuspected, and although *The Prophecy* is closer to real comedy than are the two moralities by Wilson which preceded it, it is a much more immature work than are *Locrine* and *Selimus* in conception, in choice of material, and in technique. If, however, its author was the same Robert Wilson who was collaborating on plays for Henslowe between 1598 and 1600, he must have had or later developed a strong liking for history, for of the sixteen plays for which he with others was paid, fifteen of them lost, no fewer than fourteen appear to have dealt with English or Roman history. The story of Locrine would probably have appealed to Henslowe's Robert Wilson of 1598–1600. But even if the "hellish verses" had been assigned to Robert Wilson instead of to R. W., the ascription would carry no more weight than does the ascription of selections from *Selimus* in *England's Parnassus* (1600) to Robert Greene.

42. Other instances are in the stage directions at the opening of I, i, and following lines: 174, 366, 372, 558, 769, 859, 869, 894, 906, 917, 928, 934, 997, 1180, 1536, 1579, 1633, 1678, 1714, 1732, 1755, 1766, 1773. The line numbers are those of J. Churton Collins, *Plays and Poems of Robert Greene.*

II: The True Chronicle History of Thomas Lord Cromwell

1. Algernon Charles Swinburne, *A Study of Shakespeare* (London, Chatto and Windus, 1880), p. 232.

2. Other editions of Shakespeare or of his doubtful plays which include *Cromwell* are those edited by Pope, Malone, Steevens, Theobald, Simms, Tyrrell, Hazlitt, Moltke, and finally C. F. Tucker Brooke's *The Shakespeare Apocrypha* (Oxford, Clarendon Press, 1908), upon which I have drawn in this paper for all quotations and line references.

3. August Wilhelm Schlegel, *A Course of Lectures on Dramatic Art and Literature.* Translated by J. Black (2 ed. revised, London, Bell, 1894), p. 445.

4. The dramatist permits himself to record nothing derogatory of Cromwell, whose early years were, Foxe noted, "wild and youthful, without sense or regard of God and his word, as he himself was wont ofttimes to declare unto Cranmer . . . : showing what a ruffian he was in his young days, and how he was

in the wars of the duke of Bourbon at the siege of Rome . . ."
See *Acts and Monuments,* edited by Stephen Reed Cattley (8
vols., London, 1838), V, 365. As will be noted later, the dramatist makes no mention of Cromwell's brief career as a soldier.

5. R. B. Merriman, *Life and Letters of Thomas Cromwell*
(2 vols., Oxford, Clarendon Press, 1902), II, 3–4.

6. Bandello so states, and there seems to be supporting evidence. See *Dictionary of National Biography* under Thomas
Cromwell.

7. Foxe, *Acts and Monuments,* ed. Cattley, V, 368.

8. Lines 505–12. My quotations from Drayton I have drawn
from the text in Volume II of *The Works of Michael Drayton*
edited by J. William Hebel (5 vols., Oxford, Shakespeare Head
Press, 1932).

9. Foxe, *Acts and Monuments,* ed. Cattley, V, 402.

10. Foxe, *Acts and Monuments,* ed. Cattley, V, 401.

11. Brooke, *The Shakespeare Apocrypha,* p. xxviii.

12. See pp. 10–13.

13. *The Life and Death of Thomas Lord Cromwell,* edited,
with an introduction, by A. F. Hopkinson (London, 1891), pp.
xff.; *Essays on Shakespeare's Doubtful Plays* (London, 1900),
pp. 4ff. (Each essay has separate pagination.)

14. Frederick Gard Fleay, *A Biographical Chronicle of the
English Drama, 1559–1642* (2 vols., London, Reeves, 1891),
I, 149. Dick Taylor, Jr., "Drayton and the Countess of Bedford," *Studies in Philology,* XLIX (1952), 214–28, notes that
though the final break with the Countess took place "very likely
even before 1603," when Drayton changed the dedication of
The Barons' Wars, some tributes to her remain till 1619 in later
editions of his works, probably because of the expense involved in
their removal and of the printers' desire for important names.

15. Fleay, *Biographical Chronicle,* I, 151.

16. Fleay, *Biographical Chronicle*, I, 161.

17. Arthur Acheson, *Shakespeare, Chapman and Sir Thomas More* (New York, Hackett, 1931), p. 117.

18. Acheson, *Shakespeare, Chapman*, etc., p. 255.

19. Acheson, *Shakespeare, Chapman*, etc., p. 121.

20. Acheson, *Shakespeare, Chapman*, etc., pp. 253–54.

21. How summary is Foxe's treatment is shown by the inclusion within the space of one half-page of ". . . so the freshest wits . . . sought unto him [Wolsey]; among whom was also Thomas Cromwell to his service advanced, where he continued a certain space of years, growing up in authority, till at length he was preferred to be solicitor to the cardinal. . . . Wolsey's household being dissolved, Thomas Cromwell . . . laboured to be retained into the king's service" (*Acts and Monuments*, ed. Cattley, V, 336).

22. *Dictionary of National Biography* under Essex, Robert Devereux, Earl of.

23. Historical Manuscripts Commission. Calendar of Manuscripts of the Most Hon. The Marquis of Salisbury, &c., preserved at Hatfield House, Hertfordshire. Part XIV (1923), 119.

24. Walter W. Greg, ed., *Henslowe's Diary* (2 vols., London, A. H. Bullen, 1904), II, 218.

25. Hatfield Manuscripts, XII, 248; as quoted by Edmund K. Chambers, *The Elizabethan Stage* (4 vols., Oxford, Clarendon Press, 1923), III, 248.

26. *Henslowe's Diary*, II, 218.

27. Foxe, *Acts and Monuments*, ed. Cattley, V, 395–96.

28. Edmund K. Chambers, *William Shakespeare* (2 vols., Oxford, Clarendon Press, 1930), I, 510.

29. Compare Munday's *The English Romayne Lyfe* (1582), Bodley Head Quarto, ed. by G. B. Harrison (1925), p. 2: "When as desire to see straunge Countreies, as also affection

to learne the languages, had perswaded me to leaue my natiue Countrey, . . . [I] crossed the Seas from *England* to *Bulloine* in Fraunce. From thence we trauelled to *Amiens*, in no small daunger, standing to the mercie of dispoyling Soldiers, who went robbing and killing thorowe the Countrey, the Campe beeing by occasion broken vp at that tyme. Little they left vs, and lesse would haue done by the value of our liues, had not a better bootie come then we were at that time: the Soldiers preparing towards them, whome they sawe better prouided for their necessitie: offered vs the leysure to escape, which we refused not, beeing left bare enough, bothe of coyne and cloathes."

III: The Puritan

1. Schlegel relates that "One of my literary friends, intimately acquainted with Shakespeare, was of opinion that the poet must have wished for once to write a play in the style of Ben Jonson, and that in this way we must account for the difference between the present piece and his usual manner. To follow out this idea, however, would lead to a long and very nice critical investigation." See *A Course of Lectures*, etc., translated by John Black (2d rev. ed., London, Bell, 1902), pp. 444–45.

2. Note Sergeant Puttock's speech to Pye-board, III, iv, 108: "Goe goe, little villaine, fetch thy chinck."

3. Charles W. C. Oman, *The Coinage of England* (Oxford, Clarendon Press, 1931), pp. 290–91.

4. C3 erroneously for D3. Cf. *Westward Hoe*, II, ii: "Welchmen [love] to be called Britons."

5. Walter W. Greg, ed., *Henslowe Papers* (London, A. H. Bullen, 1907), p. 105. King Christian reached England 17 July 1606 and departed 11 August.

6. Edward Arber, *A Transcript of the Registers of the Com-*

pany of Stationers of London (5 vols., London, privately printed, 1875–77), III, 308.

7. See David H. Horne, *The Life and Works of George Peele* (New Haven, Yale University Press, 1952), pp. 110–26.

8. *The Jests of George Peele* are reprinted in Volume I of A. H. Bullen's edition of Peele (2 vols., London, Nimmo, 1888) and by Horne, *Life and Works of George Peele.*

9. Quoted by and from Edward H. Sugden, *A Topographical Dictionary to the Works of Shakespeare and his Fellow Dramatists* (Manchester University Press, 1925), under Antholins (St.)

10. Wilhelm Creizenach, *The English Drama in the Age of Shakespeare* (London, Sidgwick & Jackson, 1916), p. 108.

11. (Canon) William Thompson, *The History and Antiquities of the Cathedral Church of St. Saviour (St. Marie Overie)*, 3d ed. (London, Simpkin, 1910), p. 135.

12. Anthony à Wood, *Athenae Oxonienses,* quoted from the *Dictionary of National Biography.*

13. A. F. Pollard, article on Bishop Vaughan in the *Dictionary of National Biography.*

14. Norman E. McClure, ed., *Letters of John Chamberlain* (2 vols., Philadelphia, American Philosophical Society, 1939), II, 203–04.

15. A2ᵛ.

16. Arthur T. Russell, *Memoirs of the Life and Works of . . . Lancelot Andrews* (London, 1863), p. 354, quoted from the *Dictionary of National Biography,* Art. Felton, Nicholas.

17. Thomas Fuller, *Church History of Britain,* VI, 63, quoted from the *Dictionary of National Biography.*

18. Quoted from Edmund K. Chambers, *The Elizabethan Stage* (4 vols., Oxford, Clarendon Press, 1923), IV, 249.

19. A Sermon Preached in London before the right honorable

the Lord Lawarre, Lord Gouernour and Captaine Generall of Virginia. Feb. 21, 1609 (1610); quoted from Chambers, *Elizabethan Stage*, IV, 254.

20. Chambers, *Elizabethan Stage*, II, 22.

21. A. F. Hopkinson, Essay on *The Puritan* in *Essays on Shakespeare's Doubtful Plays* (London, 1900), p. 9. (Each essay is paged separately.)

22. The broadside has been reprinted by Andrew Clark in *Shirburn Ballads* (Oxford, Clarendon Press, 1907), pp. 11–19, who notes that though the ballad had been entered at Stationers' Hall in 1597, "the present text, from the mention of James I in stanzas 23 and 40, is later than 1602–3" (p. 11). It would be interesting to know whether its reprinting preceded or followed the performance of the play.

23. "On Some Plays Attributed to Shakspere," *New Shakspere Society Transactions*, 1875–76; Part I, pp. 155–80.

24. C. F. Tucker Brooke, *Shakespeare Apocrypha* (Oxford, Clarendon Press, 1908), pp. xxxi–xxxiii.

25. See Mark Eccles, "Middleton's Birth and Education," *Review of English Studies*, VII (1931), 436–37, and Mildred G. Christian, "Middleton's Residence at Oxford," *Modern Language Notes*, LXI (1946), 90–91.

26. Wilbur D. Dunkel, "The Authorship of *The Puritan*," *Publications of the Modern Language Association of America*, XLV (1930), 804–8.

27. In *Philological Quarterly*, XXII (1943), 29–35, I have cited reasons for dating *Michaelmas Term* 1605–1606—preferably, perhaps, 1606.

IV: A YORKSHIRE TRAGEDY

1. Edward Arber, *A Transcript of the Registers of the Company of Stationers of London* (5 vols., London, privately printed,

1875–77), III, 377: "A booke called *A Yorkshire Tragedy* written by Wylliam Shakespere."

2. Arber, *Transcript*, III, 292.

3. Arber, *Transcript*, III, 295.

4. Arber, *Transcript*, III, 299.

5. John Payne Collier, ed., *Illustrations of Early English Popular Literature* (2 vols., London, privately printed, 1863–64, Vol. II, No. 11.

6. Marc Friedlaender, "Some Problems of *A Yorkshire Tragedy*," *Studies in Philology*, XXXV (1938), 238–53.

7. J. A. Venn, *Alumni Cantabrigienes* (6 vols., Cambridge, University Press, 1922–54), I, 284.

8. Joseph Foster, *Pedigrees of the County Families of Yorkshire* (2 vols., London, 1874), gives Walter's date of birth as 1571, although he notes that his father William was aged 14 on 15 December 1571 and records the date of the marriage covenant of Walter's parents as 15 November 18 Elizabeth (1576). As evidence he cites indicates that Walter was born later, the 1571 may be a typographical error for 1579. *The Calverley Register* (edited by Samuel Margerison, Bradford, 1880), although it records baptisms from 1574, contains no mention of Walter or of his many brothers and sisters until the baptism of the twins Ralph and Sheffield on 13 July 1592.

9. So suggested Thomas Dunham Whitaker, *Loidis and Elmete* (Leeds and Wakefield, 1816), footnote, pp. 228-29.

10. In "A Genealogical and Historical account of the . . . Family of Calverley of Calverley" (Item 3 in British Museum Add. MS 27,416, p. 16^v) and in Foster, *Pedigrees*, Philippa is correctly identified as "sister to John Brooke, Lord Cobham," but historians of the drama have continued to follow Whitaker, *Loidis and Elmete*, and J. S[traker], *Memoirs of the Public Life of Sir Walter Blackett . . . with a Pedigree of the Calverleys of Cal-*

verley in Yorkshire (Newcastle, 1819), in making Philippa "daughter of Sir John Brooke, son of George Brooke, Lord Cobham." The confusion is explained, of course, by the title's being in abeyance from 1603 (when Henry Lord Cobham was attainted) until 1645 when Sir John Brooke, the son of Sir Henry Cobham and the brother of Philippa, was created Baron Cobham by Charles I.

11. J.M.R. in the *Dictionary of National Biography* under Cobham, Sir Henry; and see letter of Henry Lord Cobham to Cecil, *Calendar of MSS . . . at Hatfield House,* Pt. XVII (1938), 582.

12. Historical Manuscripts Commission, *Calendar of MSS . . . at Hatfield House,* Pt. IX (1902), 186. I cannot identify Mr. Lyly. None of Walter's sisters seems to have married one of that name. Professor C. J. Sisson has suggested to me that he may have been John Lyly the dramatist, who was living in London at the time (see his *Thomas Lodge and Other Elizabethans,* Cambridge, Harvard University Press, 1933) and whose wife was from the north of England.

13. Preserved with other Calverley papers in British Museum Add. MS 27, 411. The section quoted is from fol. 8. Since this chapter was written, Mr. Glenn H. Blayney has published in *Notes and Queries* (Vol. 98, no. 8, August 1953) an excerpt from this court action, noting that in June 1598 Lady Gargrave and her son became Walter Calverley's guardians. He presumably did not know of Lady Cobham's letters.

Richard Gargrave seems to have learned little from the unhappy career of his sometime ward. Indeed, the history of the Gargrave family of the period was hardly less tragic than that of the Calverleys. Sir Thomas Gargrave, trusted soldier of Elizabeth, vice-president of the North and Speaker of the House of Commons, was upon his death in 1579 succeeded by his son Sir

Cotton Gargrave, who, after serving as High Sheriff in 1584, died four years later. Sir Cotton's heir, Thomas, who inherited the estates in 1588, was some seven years afterwards executed at York for the murder of his servant. Thomas' half-brother and heir, Sir Richard Gargrave, son of Anne and co-guardian of Walter Calverley, "was a gambler and spendthrift, and by little and little the great estates upon which he entered were parted with to support his extravagance. . . . Dodsworth wrote of him in 1634 that 'he now liveth in the Temple for sanctuary, having consumed his whole estate, to the value of 3,500 *l.* per annum at least, and hath not a penny to maintain himself but what the purchasers of some part of his lands in reversion after his mother's death allow him, in hope he will survive his mother, who hath not consented to the sale'. . . . Hunter, writing in 1830, says 'The memory of his extravagance and his vices yet lingers about Kingsley. . . . The rustic moralist still points his counsel with the story of Sir Richard Gargrave, who could once ride on his own land from Wakefield to Doncaster, and had horses innumerable, but was at last reduced to travel with the pack-horses to London, and was found dead in an old hostelry, with his head on a pack-saddle.' " See J. J. Cartwright, *Chapters of Yorkshire History* (Wakefield, 1872), pp. 84–86.

14. I do not know to which of her daughters Lady Gargrave hoped to marry Walter Calverley. One wonders if it could have been Mary, the little that is known of whose career is no less sad than that of her brother Richard. For a while she was a maid of honor to Anne of Denmark, wife of King James I. Cartwright noted that "Between the years 1631 and 1639 she presented several petitions to Charles, praying for protection against her creditors. In the first of these she stated that her pension had already been made over to them, and 'she still in much peril, having nothing to live upon.' A year later, she prayed for the renewal of

her protection, being then 1,000 *l.* in arrear 'to prevent an old servant of the King's late mother from dying miserably in prison' " (*Chapters of Yorkshire History*, p. 86).

15. *Calendar of MSS . . . at Hatfield House*, Pt. X (1904), 117.

16. *MSS . . . at Hatfield House*, p. 190.

17. The Yorkshire Archaeological and Topographical Association. Record Series, Vol. VIII. Feet of Fines of the Tudor Period, Pt. IV.

18. Inquisition post mortem, quoted by and from Whitaker, *Loidis and Elmete*, p. 221n.

19. Printed by Whitaker, *Loidis and Elmete*, p. 226n.

20. Wilkins also introduces Scarborow's uncle, Sir William Scarborow. Although Walter Calverley had no uncle named William, it may be noted that a kinsman named William Calverley served as one of Walter's guardians from March 1597 to the end of June 1598. See p. 161. Walter's father, William, did have an uncle named William Calverley.

21. *The Abridgement of the English Chronicle.* First collected by M. John Stow . . . after him augmented . . . by E. H. Gentleman, London, 1611, p. 450. The earlier account is reprinted by C. F. Tucker Brooke, *Shakespeare Apocrypha* (Oxford, Clarendon Press, 1908), p. xxxiv.

22. H. Dugdale Sykes, "The Authorship of *A Yorkshire Tragedy*," *Journal of English and Germanic Philology*, XVI (1917), reprinted in *Sidelights on Shakespeare* (Stratford-upon-Avon, Shakespeare Head Press, 1919), pp. 77–98. The quotations are from pp. 93–95.

23. I do not know what Mr. Sykes meant by "unpremeditated conclusion." Obviously the conclusion of *The Miseries* is not that of the actual incident, but Scarborow's repentance is as well motivated as is usual in treatments of the prodigal son, and no less

convincing. Compare, for instance, the sudden repentance of Flowerdale at the close of *The London Prodigal*. I can see no reason to suspect that Wilkins originally purposed to make his play a tragedy.

24. The Fleay-Sykes theory has been not only accepted but elaborated by Mr. A. M. Clark, *Thomas Heywood, Playwright and Miscellanist* (Oxford, Basil Blackwell, 1931). Noting that *The Miseries* had been described as a "tragedy" when it was entered upon the Stationers' Register, he thought "there is little reason to doubt that, together with *A Yorkshire Tragedy*, it constituted the *Four Plays in One*" (p. 307). I find a little astonishing the reasons he cites for this conviction, for he had obviously read the *Two Unnatural Murthers*. He first points out that certain characters appear in both plays: "William Scarborow and Katherine are respectively Husband and Wife. . . . Dr. Baxter is the Master of the College. . . . The uncle whom the Wife visits in London is evidently the Lord Faulconbridge," etc. (p. 307). Such parallels among the characters should obviously be expected as both plays deal with the same event and drew upon the same account; they in no way suggest that the two plays at one time constituted a single play, for, as repeatedly noted, the characters in the *Tragedy* are in every instance drawn directly from the tract. So are the situations. Mr. Clark seems to have become more confused when he further declares that "certain motifs in the *Tragedy* are begun in *The Miseries*. Thus the Husband's repeated abuse of his wife as a whore and his children as bastards results from Scarborow's protest against marrying Katherine after a precontract to Clare" (p. 309). As he is here arguing that the two plays originally constituted one, I assume that Mr. Clark's argument was that the precontract and protest must have been in an earlier form of the *Tragedy* to explain Husband's abuse of his wife and children. If such was his view, he has completely ignored the fact that the *Tragedy* agrees with

Two Unnatural Murthers, where there is no mention of a protest and no suggestion of an enforced marriage but where Calverley indulges in identical abuse. Indeed, this close agreement of the *Tragedy* and the tract, and the considered innovation in *The Miseries*, far from urging that the two plays were at one time one, argue rather that they were always separate. Mr. Clark suggests that it was the publisher Pavier, who "laying his hands on the manuscript of the discarded fifth act and one or two of the other scenes as well, suppressed the names and published the fragment as one of the *Four Plays in One*, 'called A Yorkshire Tragedy as it was plaid' " (pp. 311–12).

25. Mr. Blayney (see note 13), noting that Henry, first Lord Hunsdon, was associated with Sir Thomas Gargrave (Richard's grandfather) in affairs of the North and that his granddaughter married Henry, eighth Lord Cobham, queries whether Wilkins may not have confused the two families, Hunsdon and Gargrave.

26. Quoted from E. K. Chambers, *The Elizabethan Stage* (4 vols., Oxford, Clarendon Press, 1923), IV, 338–39.

27. Chambers, *Elizabethan Stage*, I, 96, 322.

28. Chambers, *Elizabethan Stage*, I, 303.

29. Alexander Pope, *Shakespeare* (London, J. Tonson, 1725), I, xx; J. O. Halliwell-Phillipps, *Outlines of the Life of Shakespeare* (11th ed., London, Longman, 1907), I, 223.

30. Adolphus W. Ward, *History of English Dramatic Literature* (2d ed., 3 vols., London, Macmillan, 1899), II, 231–32.

31. Algernon Charles Swinburne, *A Study of Shakespeare* (3d ed., London, Chatto and Windus, 1895), pp. 142, 144.

32. John Addington Symonds, *Shakespere's Predecessors* (London, Smith, Elder, 1884), p. 435.

33. Brooke, *Shakespeare Apocrypha*, p. xxxiv.

34. Allardyce Nicoll, *British Drama* (London, Harrap, 1925), p. 198.

35. Arber, *Transcript*, III, 377.

36. See Introduction, pp. 13–14.

37. A. M. Clark states that of the 188 plays licensed between 1584 and 1616 only 19 of the entries cite the authors (*Thomas Heywood*, p. 305).

38. Arber, *Transcript*, III, 289.

39. Arber, *Transcript*, III, 37.

40. "The Yorkshire Tragedy was pronounced by Mr. Steevens, when it was republished by Mr. Malone, in his Supplement, to have been a hasty performance by Shakspeare. This opinion, however, he seems to have silently abandoned . . ." ("Life of William Shakespeare" in Boswell-Malone edition, 1821, II, 473).

41. *A Course of Lectures on Dramatic Art and Literature.* Translated by J. Black (London, Bell, 1846), p. 445.

42. John Payne Collier, *History of English Dramatic Poetry* (London, 1879), II, 438–39.

43. Herman Ulrici, *Shakespeare's Dramatic Art.* Translated by A. J. W. M. (London, 1846), pp. 458–59.

44. How reluctantly Fleay yielded to the external evidence is shown in: "I have repeatedly . . . expressed my intense difficulty to admit that Shakespeare wrote this little play about the same time as *Lear*, in the zenith of his power . . . but the external evidence is too strong"; ". . . although I give way before this external evidence, and reluctantly admit Shakespeare's authorship . . . I have not cancelled my previous efforts to find another author." See F. G. Fleay, *Biographical Chronicle of the English Drama* (2 vols., London, Reeves, 1891), II, 206, 208.

45. F. G. Fleay, *A Chronicle History of the Life and Work of William Shakespeare* (London, Nimmo, 1886), p. 303.

46. Fleay, *Biographical Chronicle*, II, 205–6.

47. In *A Study of Shakespeare* Swinburne wrote: Shakespeare's hand, "I do not recognize even in the *Yorkshire Trag-*

edy" (p. 142); but in a much later work, *Shakespeare* (Oxford, University Press, 1909), he was hesitant to commit himself: "This is not to say that I believe it to be Shakespeare's: indeed I would rather think that impossible: but impossible I cannot quite bring myself to feel comfortably assured that it is" (pp. 42–43).

48. Ward, *History of English Dramatic Literature*, II, 231–32. Professor Tucker Brooke, however, declared that "If Shakespeare's hand is to be traced anywhere in this play, we must look for it solely in the two hundred lines of prose scattered through the first four scenes" (*Shakespeare Apocrypha*, p. xxxv).

49. Friedlaender, "Some Problems of *A Yorkshire Tragedy*," *Studies in Philology*, XXXV (1938), p. 242. Such an argument may equally well be applied to *The London Prodigal.*

50. Pope, *Shakespeare*, I, xx.

51. Edmond Malone, *Supplement to the Edition of Shakespeare's Plays, 1780*, II, 675.

52. A. R. Waller and Arnold Glover, editors, *The Collected Works of William Hazlitt* (12 vols., London, Dent, 1902–4), I, 355–57.

53. Halliwell-Phillipps, *Outlines*, I, 223.

54. Henry Tyrrell, *The Doubtful Plays of Shakespeare* (London and New York, J. Tallis, 1853), pp. 81–83.

55. Charles Knight, *Pictorial Shakspere* (8 vols., London [1843]), VII, 253–54.

56. *Cambridge History of English Literature*, V, 243.

57. Sidney Lee, *A Life of William Shakespeare* (4th rev. ed., London, John Murray, 1925), pp. 262, 404.

58. Brooke, *Shakespeare Apocrypha*, p. xxxv.

59. E. K. Chambers, *William Shakespeare* (2 vols., Oxford, Clarendon Press, 1930) I, 535.

60. Waller and Glover, editors, Hazlitt, *Works*, I, 356.

61. Clark, *Thomas Heywood*, p. 316.

62. Clark, *Thomas Heywood*, p. 317.

63. The "I am the bolder to nominate," etc., is not, I believe, indicative that the name of Calverley was used in the version of the story presented on the stage. Heywood was writing thirty years after the play had been presented, and the murderer's identity must always have been known. The arguments against the use of the names upon the stage are still valid.

64. Bertram Dobell, "The Author of 'A Yorkshire Tragedy,' " *Notes and Queries*, 10th Ser., VI (1906), 41–43. Earlier A. H. Bullen is said to have suggested Tourneur (Hopkinson, *Shakespeare's Doubtful Plays*, p. xxxii); Sir Sidney Lee (*New Shakespeare Society Transactions*, 1887–92, p. 34) suggested Heywood or Tourneur. The authorship of Thomas Middleton has also been suggested. In his discussion of the plays ascribed to Beaumont and Fletcher, the late Mr. E. H. C. Oliphant, thinking he recognized certain stylistic resemblances between Act V, scene i, of *Wit at Several Weapons* and *A Yorkshire Tragedy* ('doublings' and the same short, sharp style of sentence), declared the latter to be "a play which I am not at all sure that we do not owe to Middleton." See *The Plays of Beaumont and Fletcher* (New Haven, Yale University Press, 1927) p. 457.

65. Dobell, "The Author of 'A Yorkshire Tragedy,' " p. 43.

66. Sykes, *Sidelights on Shakespeare*, pp. 77–98.

67. Sykes, *Sidelights on Shakespeare*, p. 92.

68. E. A. Abbott, *A Shakespearean Grammar* (2d ed., London, Macmillan, 1870), Par. 244.

69. Sykes, *Sidelights on Shakespeare*, p. 82.

70. Abbott, *Shakespearean Grammar*, Par. 479.

INDEX